AMELIA

Pilot in Pearls

AMELIA

Pilot in Pearls

SHIRLEY DOBSON GILROY

LINK PRESS, PUBLISHERS

McLEAN, VIRGINIA

1985

Manufactured in the United States of America

First edition

Library of Congress Catalog Card Number: 85-50586
ISBN 0-912991-02-X

Editor: BEVERLY BOHLINGER HEGMANN

Designer: GERARD A. VALERIO, Bookmark Studio

COPYRIGHTS AND PERMISSIONS

Every effort has been made to secure proper permission for use of copyrighted works and to secure courtesy permissions as well for all material reproduced in this tribute book to Amelia.

TITLE PAGE: Photograph of Amelia Earhart given to the Smithsonian Institution by her mother in 1940. Courtesy, Smithsonian Institution.

FRONTISPIECE: This portrait of Amelia is one of several taken of her by Ben Pinchot in his Fifth Avenue Studio, New York City. Amelia is wearing her wings of Honorary Major of the 381st Air Corps Observation Squadron, now 381st Strategic Missile Wing, McConnell Air Force Base. Photograph courtesy Ben Pinchot.

FACING PAGE: Marble portrait bust of Amelia Earhart by Brenda Putnam. Courtesy, the artist's nephew Desmond O'Hara.

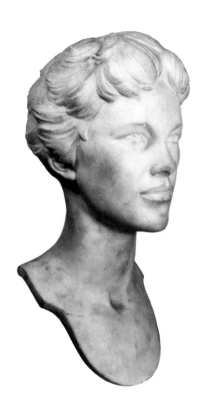

Dedicated to those whose lives

in some way have been or will be touched by

this gifted Amelia.

Into the Heavens, into the sky that was your life.
Divinely, with your wings out-spread in flight,
Climbing and seeking for a world unknown,
You vanished, like fading music, gone with the sun!

MARY HALPERIN

Contents

Foreword

People reacted to Amelia Earhart. Painters such as Howard Chandler Christy and James Montgomery Flagg painted her. David Jones cast her in bronze. Brenda Putnam chisled her in marble. The likes of Steichen captured the depths of her charm on film while poets captured the myriad facets of her personality in verse. People trapped in the day-to-day responsibilities of their lives vicariously shared her adventures.

From these pages emerges a fascinating free spirit meeting any challenge with zest and thoroughness to prove its doing. Her creative curiosity and dry wit saved many tense moments from disaster. And through it all shines her exquisite femininity. Tender of heart, yet tough of mind, this tenacious Amelia forged ahead against all odds once set on a course in which she believed. She was comfortable in the man's world she chose as her own, and was treated as a comrade by the pilots with whom she flew. A champion of women, she believed that deeds must tell the story. She took it upon herself to set an example and prove to the world, and to women themselves, that they could accomplish anything they wanted to do. She fully expected other women to follow her lead, and would have been so proud that another free spirit, Sally Ride, is the first American woman to carry her torch into outer space.

Amelia Earhart—a legend in her own time—is a heroine the world will not let die. Ahead of her time, she proved that living is an adventure for those who dare to make their dreams come true, or to grow taller in meeting the challenge.

Fay Gillis Wells

Charter Member
The Ninety-Nines

Alexandria, Virginia
1985

Preface

This book is an artistic tribute to Amelia Earhart, which sets it apart from all the biographies, technical and search-oriented volumes that have been written.

My idea for this "little volume of tributes," as it was originally envisioned, was sparked by my participation in the Commemorative Stamplift for Amelia in 1962–1963. I had already read several volumes about pioneering inroads in aviation, and was aware of the continued searches in Pacific waters for the Lockheed Electra that carried Amelia and navigator Fred Noonan. During this period, I discovered that Amelia had planned to publish an Anthology of Poetry, and I began to recognize that there were many facets of Amelia Earhart still to be explored.

My initial plan for this tribute was to include an historical retrospective, Amelia's word pictures on the beauty of flight, and writings which brought to light her sharp wit and sense of humor. This idea has been somewhat preserved, although in a different form, as the manuscript went through several revisions and any number of title changes. The "little volume" ballooned, and the voluminous correspondence extended through more years than I ever anticipated.

The tributes herein are representative of the many salutes given to Amelia. Searching for such tributes and copyright holders proved to be an educational experience. My correspondence carried me to various countries around the globe, on all of the continents, as well as to all fifty states across America.

In 1984, the last change in format and the final title was decided upon. The volume is organized into two parts: The Pilot and The Pearls. The Pilot section concerns itself with the early years, and Amelia's accomplishments and contributions to aviation. The Pearls section reveals her stature as a woman—that certain fascination—that magic that brought inspiration into the lives of men, women, and children throughout the universe. So, then, The Pilot reiterates the known—the familiar; The Pearls introduces the lesser-known aspects of Amelia Earhart.

Artists, utilizing almost every medium, have captured a glimpse of this world heroine through the eye of the camera, on canvas, on drawing boards, in bronze and clay and stone, and with their pens in poetry, prose, and song.

Also included are particular "artistic touches," as I like to call them. These were not specifically dedicated to Amelia Earhart, but might well have been inspired by her because they help to orchestrate her personality.

Biographical profiles of each artist whose tribute appears in this book, as well as of those whose "artistic touches" appear, can be found at the back of this volume, listed in alphabetical order. Unfortunately, in some cases, no information could be tracked down, although every effort was made.

Oliver Goldsmith (1728–1774) wrote: "Hope like the gleaming taper's light, adorns and cheers our way." Amelia's example, both as a pioneer and humanitarian, is still a forward light of hope to inspire us.

Here is a very special Author's Word by the late Clara Studer (1897–1979), writer and personal friend of Amelia, from her unpublished manuscript on Amelia Earhart. It expresses the sentiment of this volume:

"They shall seam the fabric of this book firmly together so that her splendid, if sometimes muted, personality may come through in honesty for all time."

S . D . G .

Manchester, Connecticut
1984

THE PILOT

Amelia before her first transcontinental flight in 1928. Determination and daring show in her face, but she is fingering her pearls.

Pilot in the Wings: The Early Years

Amelia Mary Earhart, named for her grandmothers, was born in 1897 at 223 North Terrace, Atchison, Kansas. Although there has been some controversy over her actual birthdate, this is the true date as indicated in the records of Trinity Episcopal Church in Atchison.

Since Mr. Earhart was a lawyer with the railroad, the Earhart family traveled a great deal. This instilled in young Amelia a love of travel, a reluctance to be tied down to one place, and an avid curiosity. Amelia inherited her adventuresome streak from her mother, who was the first woman to ascend all the way to the top of Pike's Peak—riding a burro part of the way and climbing on foot the rest. Amelia and her younger sister, Muriel, loved to play. They were devoted to their pets, had real concern for the welfare of all animals, and adored to ride horseback. Both parents encouraged the girls to be free spirits. At one point, Amelia and Muriel built a "Flying Dutchman" in which to play. They delightedly clambered aboard and whirled around, often hanging upside down rather than sitting demurely as was expected of young ladies at that time. Their mother made sure they were attired in appropriate playclothes that allowed these antics.

A.E.'s sister, Muriel writes:

"All nice little girls wore long full-skirted dresses with ruffled pinafores over them. . . . Mother had two suits of dark blue flannel made for us, with generous pleated bloomers gathered at the knees. We were comfortable, unconventional and entirely happy tomboys, thanks to a forward-looking mother who endured the neighbors' raised eyebrows with equanimity."

MURIEL EARHART MORRISSEY
Courage is the Price, 1963

Amelia and Muriel built a roller coaster in their yard that started eight feet in the air. Greasing the track with lard for a better ride, Amelia climbed aboard the little car. In *Courage is the Price,* Muriel recounts the story of the trial run.

Wedding Portrait, Amy Otis and Edwin Earhart, October 16, 1895. Muriel Earhart Morrissey, Amelia's sister, describes the bride's outfit as being a simple dark brown "going away" suit. The jacket, with a pinched in waist and leg o'mutton sleeves, was worn over a dressy lace blouse. The nearly-floor-length skirt had a small bustle. Her chestnut hair was topped by a feather-trimmed brown velvet toque, perched jauntily over her left eye. A fur muff and neckpiece was the finishing touch.

COURTESY: MURIEL EARHART MORRISSEY

"At one time I thought that my father must have read everything and, of course, therefore, knew everything. He could define the hardest words as well as the dictionary, and we used to try and trip him and he to bewilder us. I still have a letter he wrote me beginning, 'Dear parallelepipedon,' which sent me scurrying for a definition."

AMELIA EARHART

"After I had really flown alone, Mother was good sport enough to help me buy a small second-hand plane. . . . It happened to be the only one the builder had, so he and I worked out a scheme to use it jointly. If Mother was worried during this period, she did not show it. Possibly, except for backing me financially, she could have done nothing more helpful."

AMELIA EARHART
Fun of It, 1932

Amelia in the arms of her Aunt Margaret Otis, 1897, at the age of 5¹/₂ months. In this innocent babe lies the spirit, the determination, and the drive that would spur her on to feats of courage. She had only nine short years of flight, but the excitement she generated lived on for more than half a century. It lives on still. . . .

COURTESY: ATCHISON HISTORICAL SOCIETY

The Earhart/Otis Family Portrait. Left to Right: Muriel Earhart, Carl Otis, Grandmother Otis, unidentified, Mrs. Amy Earhart, Mr. Edwin Earhart, and Amelia (center front). Circa 1907. CREDIT: SCHLESINGER LIBRARY, RADCLIFFE COLLEGE

Amelia with her father, Edwin Earhart, Kansas City, Missouri, 1916.
Rare photograph of Amelia with long hair.

PERMISSION: HARCOURT, BRACE & JOVANOVICH

Amelia often drove her yellow Kissel "Goldbug" roadster—nicknamed The Yellow Peril because of her fondness for speed. She'd transport a carload of teenage girls from Denison House to her family home in West Milford where they'd enjoy storytelling and marshmallow roasts. Neighborhood children loved the low-slung sportscar, too. Ten or more would clamber aboard and hang on, begging to be driven "in style" past family and friends. COURTESY: MURIEL EARHART MORRISSEY

"Zoom! she went down the track. There was a sound of splintering wood and a crash as the car and passenger left the track when the car hit the trestle and tipped it over. Amelia jumped up, her eyes alight, ignoring a torn dress and bruised lip as she exclaimed happily, 'Oh, Pidge, it's just like flying!' "

Of her early years, Amelia writes,

"I loved school, though I never qualified as a teacher's pet. Perhaps the fact that I was exceedingly fond of reading made me endurable."

Because they moved around so much, Amelia attended several schools—Central High School in St. Paul, Minnesota, in 1913 and 1914. In 1915, she was graduated from Hyde Park High School, Chicago (now Hyde Park Academy). In 1916–1917, she attended Ogontz School, Rydal, Pennsylvania. Mrs. Sutherland-Brown, headmistress of that school declared, "Amelia was always pushing into unknown seas in her thinking, her reading, and in experiments in science. Her most vivid characteristic was her intellectual curiosity which burned brightly when she was with us and was certainly exemplified by her later career."

Amelia Earhart as a member of the Volunteer Aid Detachment, Canadian Red Cross, Toronto, Canada, 1917. COURTESY: MURIEL EARHART MORRISSEY

In 1919, she served as a Red Cross volunteer during World War I at Spadina Military Hospital in Toronto, Canada, with her sister Muriel. Seeking relief from the sadness that engulfed her as she helped so many armless, legless wounded led her to the airport to watch the pilots fly.

When she joined her parents in Los Angeles in 1922, her interest in flying, kindled in Canada, revived. Her father took her to the airport for her first flight, for which he paid five dollars. Famous pilot Frank Hawks took her up for the first time, but thereafter Amelia searched for a woman instructor—she was reluctant to make a mistake in front of a man.

Neta Snook took on the fledgling pilot and was a most capable instructor. ("Snooky" still lives in California today.)

Amelia loved anything that was fast and done out in the open. Flying, of course, was both. But it was expensive (for those days). Amelia had incredible persistence when it came to anything she loved. She had many, many jobs (operating a dump-truck, photography, and working for the telephone company, to name a few) in order to pay for her lessons. Further, it was necessary to ride to the end of the streetcar line and then walk four miles to get to the airport. Worst of all, she suffered greatly from a severe sinus condition, aggravated by the pressure and the open cockpit. Nothing deterred her from flying. All her life she struggled to pay for her flying; even after she became famous she kept to a grueling lecture tour, designed clothes, endorsed products, and wrote some books, as well as a column for *Cosmopolitan* for a period of one and a half years.

After the failure of her parents' marriage, she and her mother drove to Boston in her bright canary yellow roadster, most appropriately nicknamed "The Yellow Peril"—not merely for its color, but because its speed-loving owner was fond of hurtling around town (more often than not with a carload of laughing young charges from Denison House). Amelia's first plane was a lovely chrome yellow. She liked to explain that this was also a safety feature—should she come down in the sea, it would be easy to spot bobbing in the waves.

Amelia became a social worker at Denison House at 93 Tyler Street in Boston. It was there that she was discovered by George Palmer Putnam, a public relations man working on behalf of Amy Phipps Guest, a wealthy pilot from Pittsburgh who wanted to become the first woman pilot to cross the Atlantic. When Mrs. Guest encountered opposition from her family, she set out to seek another "Lady Lindy." It was then that Amelia came to her attention.

It's interesting that Amelia did not begin flying until she was in her twenties. At first she thought she might become a doctor, but found that too confining. She liked her freedom. When she was in one place too long, she felt like a bird in a cage. Her travel as a child instilled in her a wanderlust that kept her seeking adventure in her later years.

Amelia Earhart would have made an excellent scientist. She thrived on her science courses in colleges. Professor MacGregor, who taught her biology, reminisces:

> *"She was a most stimulating student. . . . I felt that had Amelia not become caught up in the adventure of flying, she would have found equally challenging frontiers to conquer in the laboratory."*

> *Courage is the Price*, p. 115

It was the time that she devoted to exploring areas of study, trying many different jobs and giving thoughtful consideration to many different subjects and interests, that broadened her and made her a much richer person when she finally found her path.

Amelia was embarrassed by the accolades she received for her participation in the 1928 Friendship Flight. She felt that they were undeserved, since she was "just" a passenger. She was determined to make sure that she would deserve that acclaim; it motivated her to accept all challenges that came her way. She never made a fuss about the feats she planned to

A. E. and George Palmer Putnam on their Rye, New York estate. Amelia said of him, "My husband, a practicing believer in wives doing what they do best, is an approving and helpful partner in all my projects." COURTESY: MURIEL EARHART MORRISSEY

attempt. No one knew her intentions until she was already in the air. Although she loved flying, her drive came from a desire to see women proved capable of all things that men could do—in fact, most of the records she set were records that men had not yet accomplished. While she was at Purdue, she insisted that a room be set aside—"Tinkering for Women Only"—where women could go to experiment with motors and equipment. She felt it was very difficult for women to make inroads in aviation and other "men's" fields—there were so many ingrained "do's and don'ts" to deal with. It was *unseemly* for women to do thus and such; it was *in poor taste* to do this or that. But Amelia was well prepared to break these taboos—she had broken many as a child. Her bloomers as a seven-year old paved the way for the slacks and touseled hair of the pilot.

Ironically, the world flight on which she went down was to have been her final aviation effort. She felt that when she had achieved that, she would have done all that she could do. Hers was not an all-consuming passion to fly, but, rather, a determination to prove that women were capable of great feats of courage, and had the intelligence and technical expertise to do whatever it was that they wanted to do.

Never-before-published studio photograph of Amelia, circa 1922. COURTESY: ATCHISON HISTORICAL SOCIETY – KANSAS CITY SHOWCASE

Amelia with her Lockheed Electra.

Taking Wing:
The Years of Flight and Fancy

Perhaps the strangest thing about this art of the sky is its power over the soul. RICHARD LeGALLIENNE

Amelia Earhart was a courageous lady who looked to the skies and beyond—and saw no limits. A woman of foresight and vision, she was not confined by horizons—she saw into space in 1934! Dwight D. Eisenhower spoke of her as being "alone in the universe and unafraid." In fact, Amelia totally enjoyed herself. Indeed, leaving security behind, she ventured forth to set significant records in aviation.

The most noted flights include the 1928 trans-Atlantic flight from Trespassey Bay, Newfoundland, to Burry Port, Wales, in the Fokker seaplane *Friendship* with Wilmer Stultz, Pilot; Lou Gordon, Mechanic; and Amelia as passenger—the first woman to cross the Atlantic in an airplane. On May 20–21, 1932, in a Lockheed Vega powered by a single Pratt & Whitney Wasp engine, she became the first woman to fly solo across the Atlantic from Harbour Grace, Newfoundland. Her destination was to have been Paris, but mechanical problems set her down in Culmore, Ireland.

On January 11–12, 1935, again in a Lockheed Vega powered by a single Pratt & Whitney Wasp engine, Amelia Earhart became the first person to solo across the Pacific waters from Honolulu to Oakland, California. In this same year, on April 19–20, she made the first solo flight ever from Burbank, California, to Mexico City—a good-will flight. On May 8th, Amelia completed the first non-stop solo flight from Mexico City to Newark, New Jersey.

In 1937, in a Lockheed Electra powered by Pratt & Whitney engines, her first world flight was attempted. The crew consisted of Amelia Earhart, Pilot; Paul Mantz, Co-Pilot; Harry Manning, Navigator; and Fred Noonan, Navigator. The first leg of the journey from Oakland to Honolulu was successful. But a tire blew on takeoff from Honolulu, causing damage to the fuselage. Unfortunately, the flight had to be delayed until the plane could be taken back to the mainland and repaired.

On June 1, 1937, Amelia attempted the world flight a second time, taking off from Miami Airport. This was the first world flight near the equator. On July 2nd, the Lockheed

Left to Right: Betty Wyler Gillies, A. E., Frances Marsalis, Elvy Kalep (first civilian pilot in Estonia).
Roosevelt Field, New York, 1933. COURTESY: COLLECTION, BETTY WYLER GILLIES

Electra, bearing Amelia Earhart, Pilot, and Fred Noonan, Navigator, went down in Pacific waters near Howland Island.

Of Amelia and her premature death in 1937, much has been written:

In an editorial in *The Watchman-Examiner:*

> *"On the wings of a great adventure, she flew beyond the rim of this world's horizon . . . whatever circumstances one might find her, she was always the courteous spirit, unobtrusive, gentle of voice, full of humor but capable of feminine dignity and serious thought and speech."*

From editorial writer Francis J. Cummings in *Blade and Ledger,* this:

> *"Amelia Earhart was never over-powered by the fame attending her achievements in aviation."*

Her friend, pilot Louise Thaden, leaves us these words:

> *"There will never be another like her, and I am sure she will stand forever unique among the taller women pilots."*

A. E. ready to participate in the first National Woman's Air Derby, which lasted for eight grueling days. In this event, Amelia gained valuable training for her solo trans-Atlantic flight. COURTESY: NATIONAL AIR AND SPACE MUSEUM, SMITHSONIAN INSTITUTION

A. E. in flying clothes after her solo flight, Newfoundland, 1932. CREDIT: NEWFOUNDLAND PROVINCIAL MUSEUM

The Resonance of History is neither in the keening of the crowd nor in the thunder of conquerors, but in the heartbeats of the handful who skirmish in the lonely unknown beyond security.

The medium of their adventure may be the cloistered halls of scholarship, the laboratories of science, the depths of the sea, the expanse of geography, the infinity of space; but they are one in challenging the limitations imposed by ignorance and fear.

In their day they may be idolized or ignored, crowned or crucified, but only in the perspective of time can they be measured.

To the evolution of human progress came in due course the first crude tools of flight, and the hitherto segregated abode of the Gods became available to men. With characteristic cynicism the heavens soon were made the most sanguine of battlegrounds. The ultimate blessing of the wing was obscured in the curse of conflict. Only the few sensed or cared that the forged weapon was a catalyst of the open road.

In the aftermath of war such utilizations as air mail and transport were inaugurated, and exploration of the far places became a romance. Notable flights fitfully stirred public imagination, but aviation remained a business for heroes—a roulette of the reckless.

Into this impasse of apathy strode a long-legged girl. Taking no advantage of her femininity, she picked up achievements of the heroes—flew the continent non-stop—spanned the North Atlantic—cruised the Pacific from Hawaii to the Golden Gate—and in numberless sorties hither and yon set aviation in a framework of distaff acceptability.

A scant ten years were hers before she disappeared forever in the reaches of the Pacific, her globe-girdling objective almost within grasp; but in that decade she left indelible reminders that life is not a span of time but of spirit.

Before Amelia, other women had flown from earliest days—flown brilliantly with frail apparatus. Their places are secure in aviation history. Since Amelia, still others have been pilots of great distinction. Their places, too, are firm to fame. However, it was hers to serve at a time when her flying spanned a chasm between grim skepticism and the realization of new freedom. 'For the Fun of It,' she said. Nor will any who measure life in spirit rather than time deny that the long lonely hours, the uncertainty and fear, the incessant toil to attain professional skills—yes, even the ditching short of the destination—is not too great a price for the 'fun' of it.

Although Amelia belongs to all the people and to history, in a special sense she belongs to us airmen. During her life she gave and received the same open-handed comradeship that airmen give one another. When she went down, her obituary among us was the same, 'damn the luck' that we muttered in loss of each other.

GILL ROBB WILSON

TODAY AND TOMORROW

AMELIA EARHART

BY WALTER LIPPMANN

I cannot quite remember whether Miss Earhart undertook her flight with some practical purpose in mind, say to demonstrate something or other about aviation which will make it a little easier for commercial passengers to move quickly around the world. There are those who seem to think than an enterprise like hers must have some such justification, that without it there was no good reason for taking such grave risks.

But in truth Miss Earhart needs no such justification. The world is a better place to live in because it contains human beings who will give up ease and security and stake their own lives in order to do what they themselves think worth doing. They help to offset the much larger number who are ready to sacrifice the ease and the security and the very lives of others in order to do what they want done. No end of synthetic heroes strut the stage, great bold men in bulletproof vests surrounded by squads of armed guards, demonstrating their courage by terrorizing the weak and the defenseless. It is somehow reassuring to think that there are also men and women who take the risks themselves, who pit themselves not against their fellow beings but against the immensity and the violence of the natural world, who are brave without cruelty to others and impassioned with an idea that dignifies all who contemplate it.

The best things of mankind are as useless as Amelia Earhart's adventure. They are the things that are undertaken not for some definite, measureable result, but because someone, not counting the costs or calculating the consequences, is moved by curiosity, the love of excellence, a point of honor, the compulsion to invent or to make or to understand. In such persons mankind overcomes the inertia which would keep it earthbound forever in its habitual ways. They have in them the free and useless energy with which alone men surpass themselves.

Such energy cannot be planned and managed and made purposeful, or weighed by the standards of utility or judged by its social consequences. It is wild and it is free. But all the heroes, the saints and the seers, the explorers and the creators, partake of it. They do not know what they discover. They do not know where

Amelia Earhart, North Hollywood, California. Circa 1934.
CREDIT: SCHLESINGER LIBRARY, RADCLIFFE COLLEGE

their impulse is taking them. They can give no account in advance of where they are going or explain completely where they have been. They have been possessed for a time with an extraordinary passion which is unintelligible in ordinary terms.

No preconceived theory fits them. No material purpose actuates them. They do the useless, brave, noble, the divinely foolish and the very wisest things that are done by man. And what they prove to themselves and to others is that man is no mere creature of his habits, no mere automaton in his routine no mere cog in the collective machine, but that in the dust of which he is made there is also fire, lighted now and then by great winds from the sky.

Taken prior to Amelia's last flight, 1937, by Clyde Sunderland. COURTESY: PURDUE UNIVERSITY LIBRARIES—SPECIAL COLLECTIONS

18

AMELIA, ON AVIATION:

In a radio address over the National Broadcasting Company in 1930, A.E. expressed these thoughts: "A few years ago, one had to be a good sport to undertake air travel of any kind. The airplanes used were small and light and open to all kinds of weather. Landing fields were dirty and there were no facilities whatsoever for any kind of comfort. . . ."

In a 1935 radio speech, Amelia referred to aviation as "this modern young giant," further stating that "no other phase of modern progress contrives to maintain such a brimming measure of romance and beauty coupled with utility as does aviation." In an undated article, entitled, "What Flying Is Teaching Women" by A.A. Preclado, A.E. predicted that "Aviation is going to change the character of our home life as much as the automobile has done in the past few years."

"Considered off hand, travel falls into two classes—one where there is the excitement of exploration and the other where the territory has become routine . . . I have often watched daily riders and have yet to observe one gazing with animation out of the window at the same objects he has seen time and again before. In fact, most of them sit buried in a paper or book or their thoughts and only look about when they wish to discover how far they are from their tiresome journey's end. . . ."

AMELIA EARHART
November 1930, from an article,
"The Most Troubled Road,"
The National Aeronautic

There is no question that the Kansan Amelia Mary Earhart was ahead of her time, judging by her progressive ideas and by her pioneering efforts in air transportation.

On June 2, 1935, in Prospertown, New Jersey, Amelia tested a parachute device which Naval officials from the parachute school at Lakehurst felt would be valuable for purposes of student instruction.

A. E. standing under stepladder at the airfield.
COURTESY: NATIONAL AIR AND SPACE MUSEUM, SMITHSONIAN INSTITUTION

In 1936, she tested a fog-dispelling compound with a device operated by C.R. Pleasants of San Francisco, who invented it. The test took place near Union Air Terminal at Burbank, California.

She was an organizer of the National Glider Association, which also included Eddie Rickenbacker and Wolfgang Klemperer.

Former Superintendent of Oakland International Airport, Fred McElwain, who saw her off from Oakland on her first world flight attempt, said of her:
"She is deserving of all the praise that is possible to give her. No one person or aviator gave more to aviation than she did."

Igor Sikorsky, inventor, writer, and engineer, wrote of her:
"I believe that in the difficult and hazardous days of long-distance flying, not many strong or experienced men were able to contribute as much as Amelia Earhart had contributed during her all-too-short career and life."

AMELIA AND THE AUTOGIRO

On April 8, 1931, Amelia Earhart established an official altitude record in an Autogiro. The Autogiro, a forerunner of the helicopter, could take off vertically in about the same space required by the helicopter.

"It seems to me whether or not the Autogiro ever invades the general field of aeronautical activity that one of its accomplishments—that of hovering in the air under certain conditions—will be utilized for special work. Perhaps it will be found especially adaptable in aerial photography.

AMELIA EARHART, 1932

It is interesting to note that the Autogiro has been restored and was flown in the early 1980's. A Pitcairn Autogiro like the one Amelia Earhart flew is also being restored.

An incident AE enjoyed describing concerned the time a sandstorm forced a landing in the midst of a desert eighteen miles from Loveland, Nevada. Eddie Gorksi, her mechanic, was with her, for the temperamental 'giro required constant expert grooming. To city-bred Eddie, who had never been West, the great open spaces did not appeal, and he was thoroughly unhappy and lonely as he and his employer staked down the 'giro and sat on its tail to keep the contraption from blowing away.

When the worst of the wind had passed, AE wiped the sand from her eyes and mouth.

'Eddie, did you notice that house as we came down?' Eddie disconsolately shook his head.

'I haven't seen a house in three days,' he said.''

GEORGE PALMER PUTNAM
from *Soaring Wings*

AMELIA'S INTEREST IN "YOUNGER WINGS:"

That Amelia Earhart was an inspiration to people of all ages, from all stratas of life, is obvious when we look at the myriads of tributes heaped upon her and read the wonderful words written about her accomplishments. But perhaps of all those she motivated to do all that they could do, it would please her most to know how children reacted to her.

Alice Rogers Hager dedicated her book *Wings to Wear* to A. E. in this manner:

"This book is dedicated to Amelia Earhart, still First Lady of the Air, because she was always ready to point the way to young wings that ached for the sky."

Amelia, herself, wrote this Foreword for the book *Air Babies,* written and illustrated by Elvy Kalep, the first civilian pilot in her native Estonia:

"When last I surveyed the field of children's aviation literature, I found very, very little indeed for the very young. Yet everyone in the industry knows this extremely youthful group is the most important of all the citizenry as concerns airplanes and air travel. They take both so entirely for granted that while they sometimes nonplus their complex-ridden elders, they are the pride and joy of 'Aeronauts' . . .
May these two—Air Babies and Children—prove warm friends."

That Amelia was successful in stimulating the interest and curiosity of "younger wings" is evidenced in these letters and essays from Michigan school children in 1935. In all cases, these are reproduced as written, with permission from Purdue University Libraries, West Lafayette, Indiana, where they are on file.

AMELIA EARHART—Her Contribution to Aviation.

As aircraft is one of the outstanding products of creative genius in the twentieth century, so is Amelia Earhart one of the foremost characters connected with it.

Her many first woman flights have proven that women can pilot planes, of every description as safely as men.

However, since she was the first person to cross the Pacific Ocean from Honolulu, encountering several hazzards while doing so, and also the first to solo from Mexico City to New York, these are perhaps two of her greatest achievements for aviation. They open newer and faster lanes for passenger and freight

Amelia Earhart in the PCA-2 Autogiro, forerunner of the helicopter. Pitcairn Field, Willow Grove, Pennsylvania, 1931.

service. She also opened several other shorter routes. Her untiring efforts and courage have helped to commercialize aircraft.

In the history of aviation, many famous . . . have given their talents and skill to the cause, yet none have achieved greater things . . . than Amelia Earhart.

Jean Campbell, Grade 8 B, Age 12.

Amelia Earhart is probably the most unique personality in modern aviation. She is the pioneer of her sex in the air. She has squarely put it up to the men that women's place is not only in the home but above the clouds.

Not chattering like most females, but proves her point.

Being such a successful competitor she offers a continual challenge to the bird-man.

We will not name her many air achievements, they are too well known and undoubtedly appreciated. But more admirable and better to be mentioned here is the dogged stick-to-itiveness that Columbus showed in *his* Atlantic crossing. Such character as these pioneers have shown, makes me proud to be an American. We should not be discouraged for America is still producing dauntless trail blazers.

Not like Alexander, crying for more worlds, for she has found new worlds and conquered them, and wings her way, Calling to us on the ground "CONTACT."

Charles Cole, Age 15, Grade 9

Amelia Earheart says she thinks the most important thing a person can do is try herself out. Amelia Earheart does not fly for thrills or stunts, but for convenient means of transportation. She is interested in furthering this plan. To do what Miss Earheart did, you must have courage. She, we all know, has made a new record in the experiments with her autogiro, as well as being the first woman to fly across the Atlantic. She has been a commercial photographer, a worker in a telephone company, a social worker, a Red Cross Aid, a teacher, and now an aviator. Into each experience she has thrown herself in keen zest. If we all tried ourselves out as Miss Earheart did, perhaps some of us would have jobs in which we could be successful.

Mary Hobson, Grade 8 A, Age 12

How do you like Port Huron? I dont know what to say. I'm so excityd. I've never been in an airplane and just think I'm writing to a real live aviator.

Is it fun to fly up in the air?

Our teacher say you might take one of us up in your airplane, so I hope Im spelling my words wright.

I don't think I be able to come to the show to see you because it cost too much, but I hope I'll be one of the lucky children to go for a ride.

I don't think Port Huron will . . . seem very exciting to you after you have been . . . all over the world but I hope you will have a good time and come again some time If you come . . . the summer and like to go swimming we have a very good place for that.

I hope I will see you next Tuesday.

Billy Krinkle, Age 9

A poem entered my mind when I sat by the radio in my reading chair attempting to begin my essay.

Philip James Bailey had written "Life" as follows: "We live in deeds, not years; in thoughts, not breaths; In feelings, not in figures on a dial. We should count time by heart-throbs. He most lives who thinks most, feels the noblest, and acts the best."

A half an century ago, men would war with Science, to conquer the unknown. Later, as years went by, perhaps Amelia then a girl, wondered what it was like above those clouds? Or wondered if she, would ever have an opportunity to find out.

Father Time perhaps read her childhood thoughts and watched o'er her until the day had come for Amelia to conquer something she had little knowledge of. Amelia, fearless and bravely held the control stick which had guided her to fame.

To mention several of Miss Earhart's great achievements and honors: The first American woman to receive the Distinguished Flying Cross, The first woman to fly across the Atlantic, and the first woman to receive the National Geographic Society's gold medal.

She, like Washington, was the First in the hearts of her countrywomen and countrymen and as a result of her air career, a great name has rested upon the lips of american children, and a donor to the field of Science.

Shirley J. Monroe

Amelia Earhart, who made the first trans-atlantic flight on record in nineteen hundred and twenty-eight, did not know what dangers she was going to encounter. She has performed a task which no other woman has ever attempted or even thought of doing. In fact, she has not only flown over the Atlantic Ocean, but has also flown over the United States in an autogyro plane.

This woman had to make many sacrifices to become the great world-wide known flier that she is today. She took her first lesson in a city near Los Angeles, California where she lived with her father. In order to continue her lessons in flying she had to pawn some of her jewelry and her fur coat.

She has succeeded very well in her long flights, two of which were solo, and she has interested many young women of today in aviation.

Luella Semrow, Age 15

Amelia, upon having set an altitude record of 14,000 feet at an air meet, had this to say to her sister, Muriel, and her father:

"It was such fun just flying through the clouds, I felt like climbing higher and higher . . ."
MURIEL EARHART MORRISSEY
Courage is the Price, 1963

In final form, flight charts are really lovely things. On them are drawn the compass courses, with their periodic changes, distances, airports and the like. As supplementary data accumulate, marginal notes assume encyclopedic proportions—details about airports, service facilities, prevailing winds, characteristics of local weather and terrain, critical altitudes, emergency landing possibilities, and much besides.
AMELIA EARHART
Last Flight, 1937

A. E. carrying maps of her projected flight in the 1935 Bendix Race, Burbank Airport (now Hollywood-Burbank Airport). Photograph by Charles Carter.

COURTESY: COLLECTION, DUSTIN CARTER

24

BALLAD OF AMELIA EARHART
1897–1937

BY WILLIAM ROSE BENÉT

SHE was a free spirit. She loved the air
As men have loved sea. In the air all was well.
Now endless empty ocean . . . nothing there
But the slow Pacific swell,

The blaze of sun where alien islands are strewn,
Towering horizon cloud, rain seething water white,
Palm and brittle eucalyptus rustling to the moon,
Mysterious tropic night.

She came to the loneliest sea, the sky most lone,
The last hazard. She mounted from the New Guinea shore
On a final course no man had ever flown
In the story of flight before.

For Howland Island headed the silver spread
Of the long twin-motored *Electra,* a fleck of land
Far in the South Pacific; and overhead
Invisible shadow moved like a closing hand.

The ships set watch, far-scattered on the sea.
The night listened. Ocean waited the word.
The pulse of their own hope that was not to be
Seemed a drone on high that they heard.

Then blank dawn. The search without avail.
Hope abandoned at last. The banners of summer furled.
Somewhere beyond all hailing ended the trail
That nearly had girdled the world.

She was a free spirit, one with the sun,
And worked for the foreign poor, and her heart beat
Valiant—as ever it throbbed to a flight begun—
For the children of Tyler Street,

Chinese and Syrian, swarming the car she loved,
"The Yellow Peril"—clamorous for a drive—
The girl of the west laughing, because she approved
Young faces alert and alive.

Friendly to all the people of her land;
The men of the hangars liked her cheerful way.
"Happy out on the tarmac, ready to lend a hand,
She knew her ship!" said they.

In a western college teaching its youth to fly,
A workshop planned for girls of mechanical mind—
And always that whisper of beauty high and deep in the sky,
Beauty she flew to find.

Slim, tousle-headed, blonde, with a straight blue gaze,
Humorous mouth, and a will no toil could tire,
Spare her the elegies now, the flowery praise,
Who had her heart's desire!

First, the summer of Nineteen Twenty Eight,
The tri-motored Fokker *Friendship,* northward driven
In the very month of the polar *Italia's* fate,
Circles the Newfoundland heaven,

Pontoons having lifted in a burst of spray
That cut the engines—they catch—and roaring free
Shake off the drag of many days delay
And thunder away to sea.

Steadied by Stultz like a steed for the ocean run,
With a strong wind blowing and driving abaft her beam
The great plane soars with three, and of them one
Whose early and girlish dream

As a tyro flier seems miracle come true,
Though she rides but to keep the log and watch and wait . . .
Through the first long hour in the bright clear they flew.
Then they saw the fog create

A lost world where cumulus creatures of cloud
Reared monster heads. The radio signaled, calling.
Three tons of airplane hurtled aloft aloud,
Nosed down, they were rising, falling,

Were bucking headwind and rain—and the sun sank
In a hazed horizon of fog, and rainbows grew
Evolved by the propellers, and the deep cloud-bank
Loomed like iceberg; rosy light shone through

Till, like the Mojave Desert, in cloudy grain
Plateaus of mist emerged; through darkening shrouds
Only the glowing exhausts of the flying plane—
For nineteen hours only a sea of clouds!

Read in the Earhart log! No sense of duty
Scrawled those pages. Ever again they sing:
"I knelt by the chart-table gulping beauty!"
"A mountain of fog, the North Star tipped our wing."
"'Dawn the rosy-fingered'!"

                             Dragons in the morning sun
The clouds reared. Now plummeting dove the plane,
Sighted a liner, circled, the journey well-nigh done;
With radio dead, sought for reply in vain.

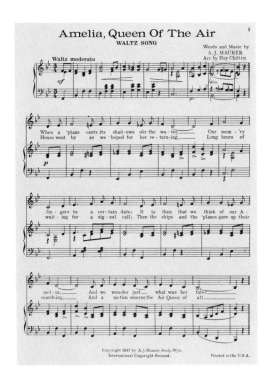

"Amelia, Queen of the Air," Words and Music by A. J. Mauer, Arrangement by May Chittim. PERMISSION: MARY MAURER MAUCH

All craft were thwart their course; they could not understand!
And then, they were striking cliffs where waves were beating
And roads and fields flowed in on either hand.
A channel they followed flashed—there was no retreating—

Stultz set her down on an estuary's reach.
Freed from their small-walled world of fog-clogged air,
The gilt wings bobbed at a buoy . . . they saw a beach . . .
Men working at a railroad over there . . .

Burry Port in Carmarthenshire, in Wales!
"First Woman to Cross the Atlantic Through the Sky."
Spite of her words, the wild fanfare prevails,
She the least of the three: "Bill, Slim, and I."

Then four years pass—of autogiro flight,
Speed in a Lockheed, span of a continent,
Airline promotion, daring of desert night—
And now, long weighed and pondered, her intent

Is an Atlantic solo. A *Vega* three years old
But newly engined—a gallant ship to con—
Guided by Bernt Balchen leaves the fold
At Hasbrouck Heights, flies in four hours to St. John

With hurried Amelia; and next to Harbour Grace
Where Balchen and the mechanic test for strain
The *Vega's* every part, that Earhart race
The dark Atlantic with a perfect plane.

"Okay! So-long; good luck!" A night of May
Five years since Lindbergh's flight. She takes the sky
Into the sunset, upon her lonely way.
At first, fair weather; a moon to profit by,

And then the altimeter uncontrolled
Swung loose, and through a broken weld came flames
From the exhaust collector's manifold,
And midnight brought black storm playing its games

With violence she had never known before;
Then calmer weather, and cloud through which to climb—
And forming ice, and the tachometer
Spinning its dial—and in a second's time

The plane was in a spin—three thousand feet
It dove! The ice melted. Flying control
Was fought for—won—out of the slush and sleet
Almost into the waves! But the ship's soul

Shuddered, responded like a living thing.
Then, with the gyro compass, she flew blind
For hours; at dawn saw, like a fluttering wing,
Wild blowing foam, which meant a northwest wind;

Sailed above cloud like snow-fields. (Dogwood blossoms
Of home came to her mind!) The sun shone through
Dazzling her eyes. So, into white cloud bosoms
She plunged, and under cloud, and the last hour or two

With the manifold shaking flame and a gauge leaking,
She flew low—found a shore—followed its line,
Turned north; and at last such field as she was seeking
Showed underwing . . .

        The red plane scattered the bellowing kine!

Earhart slid the hatch, stood up, and said to a man
Approaching, "I'm from America. Can you tell—?"
"Where you are?" he answered, "Well then, that I can!
You're down in Gallagher's pasture!"

Or, as it befell,
Five miles from Londonderry. Some seven hours
Less than her time in the *Friendship*. Now at last
By herself, alone, she had dared the plotting powers
Of night and storm, and knew all peril past.

All peril past? No! "Courage is the price
That life exacts for peace," wrote the undaunted flier.
Ever the new horizon, ever the old device
Of challenge on the helm, the goal set higher.

Lone across the Pacific next she flew
On high from Honolulu, another night of nights.
Six thousand feet, and the water darker blue
Then black, and then she was flashing her landing lights

To a pinkish glow below, a ship unseen.
Rain squalls and moon-set; now with the stars alone
She pondered her husband's voice, how near and clear had been
That radio from the Coast! Now she had flown

Into the dawn, a shadow of light that played
Round the horizon. Swiftly the stars were dying.
To her happy heart she murmured undismayed,
"The lure of beauty is the lure of flying." . . .

And then again, over the great high valley
Where Mexico City lay, after another flight,
She saw the ageless ranges meet and rally
Where the ancient volcano lifts its snow-crowned height,

And dared the Gulf due north and flew, homing,
The seven hundred miles of daylight sea,
And knew in her heart her heart wedded to roaming,
Her home the element that made her free.

So the last landfall! All that marvelous finding
Across the world; the miracle of days;
White Caribbean cities in sunlight blinding,
Venezuela jungle waterways,

The props a blur in the flight to Senegal
When the wide heavens opened with tons of rain;
Deep Africa, the Niger, and the sprawl
Of vast Lake Chad; the marabou and crane,

The beehive huts, the blacks; strange Hadramaut;
Across Arabia from the far Red Sea;
Monsoons, terrific rain; all she had sought
In her childhood dreams, suddenly coming to be!

The flashing golden pagoda of Rangoon,
The mauve sea down the shoreline of Malay;
Singapore, Java, Timor Sea, too soon
Port Darwin in Australia—all the way

The heart exulting, the heart beating, beating:
This is the beautiful world; if I die flying
This is to know the world. Let time be fleeting;
I have seen, I have known, I have no fear of dying!

And the voice heard . . . over the leagues of air
Always the loved voice, strengthening, understanding.
We live forever when the Voice is there . . .
She was born for the air.

This was a "Happy Landing."

Amelia Earhart, Cleveland Air Races, August 29th to September 7th, 1931. CREDIT: OFFICIAL U.S. AIR FORCE PHOTOGRAPH

Of Amelia's lecture endeavors, George Palmer Putnam recounts this vignette in *Soaring Wings:*

> After a lecture, a communicative mama who barged up to her resolutely buttonholed her, saying, "Do you know what my little boy said about your lecture here today?" "No," said AE, "what did your little boy say?" "Well, he saw your picture beside the box office and he came home crying, 'Mommy, Mommy, Colonel Lindbergh's mother is going to speak at the theatre!' "

Muriel tells us that Amelia loved the sound of a purring engine. Once while watching a mechanic tune up her engine, she was elated when a sputter turned to a pulsating roar. She "danced a little jig of joy, clasped both hands over her head, expressing her gratitude and admiration to the grinning, grease-smeared genius by a little bow. She came over to me and above the deafening sound, she shouted, "Beautiful symphony, what?"

ONLY BAGGAGE

(Miss Amelia Earhart, after her record-making trip by airplane from America to Great Britain, used these words to describe her participation in the flight.)

Only baggage? If we grant it,
    Ah, what precious freight was there!
Mother-courage, child-eyed wonder,
    Maiden spirit pure and fair,
With the whole world as her suitor—
    Atlanta of the Air!

Not a sordid thought went with her,
    Just the new pride of the West—
She, a letter writ to Europe,
    though it bore not crown or crest,
With nobility envisaged
    As the best of all our best.

Take her England, to your hearthstone!
    Harbor, France, her flying feet!
'Tis a woman's soul we send you
    Stronger than a friendly fleet;
And remember, in your welcome
    'Tis America you greet.

             ROBERT UNDERWOOD JOHNSON

June 19, 1928.

"Lady Lindy" was first played in Madison Square Garden in 1928 with Harold Levey conducting. COPYRIGHT, 1928

1928 FRIENDSHIP FLIGHT

(Tresspassey Bay, Newfoundland, to Burry Port, Wales)

First crossing of the Atlantic by a seaplane: Fokker F. VIIB-3M,

Crew:

Wilmer Stultz, Pilot; Lou Gordon, Mechanic; Amelia Earhart, Passenger

"When we landed at Burry port, my entire baggage consisted of two scarfs, a toothbrush and a comb. One scarf was quickly snatched by some enthusiast, I don't know just when. The other stayed with me because it happened to be tied on."

             AMELIA EARHART
             Fun of It

Of the Friendship flight, Amelia writes:

"Originally the Fokker was a land plane with wheels but pontoons had been built and fitted so that it was transformed into a seaplane, the first tri-motor so equipped. The motors to carry the Fokker were Wright Whirlwinds, 225 horsepower each. The width of the wings of the ship was about 72 feet, which is more than twice as broad as most houses are high. They were painted a lovely gold and narrowed gracefully in shape at the tips. The body of the ship, the fuselage, was orange, which blended beautifully with the gold. It was chosen however, not for artistic effect, but because chrome-yellow, its technical name, can be seen farther than any other color. In case we had to come down, a little bright spot bobbing about on the water would have stood a better chance of attracting attention than one of neutral tints."

1932 SOLO FLIGHT OF AMELIA EARHART

(Harbour Grace, Newfoundland, to Culmore, Ireland)

Newspaperman Stewart Sheppard in conversation with A. E., Harbour Grace, 1932. Photograph by R. T./W. E. Parsons. PERMISSION: WILLIAM PARSONS

May 19, 1932—Left New York at 2:30 p.m. E.S.T. (Eastern Standard Time), arrived at St. John, New Brunswick, at 6:46 p.m. Left St. John, New Brunswick at 7:30 a.m., E.S.T., May 20th; passed Port aux Basques at 12:14 p.m.; Grand Bruit at 12:20 p.m.; Recontre East at 1:25 p.m.; Heart's Delight at 1:55 p.m., and arrived at Harbour Grace at 2:00 p.m., May 20th, 1932. Refueled, with assistance disembarked, and Mrs. Putnam announced Atlantic hop would be attempted solo.

At 7:25 p.m. plane hopped off from Harbour Grace. Following morning, May 21st, 1932, Londonderry, Ireland reported plane made forced landing there with manifold exhaust trouble; time not given. This is the first Trans-Atlantic lady solo flight. No air mail taken. Miss Earhart at Harbour Grace same time as German Do X seaplane at Dildo enroute to Europe.

The NEWFOUNDLAND QUARTERLY

A Recollection of Miss Amelia Earhart by Newfoundland newsman, F. Burnham Gill:

"I can see her now, busy directing the refuelling operations, using the head of an oil barrel as a prop to write numerous cablegrams and to spread out the weather reports that were arriving in a steady flow. Later she walked all over the area charming the young people as she stopped to chat with them and to tell them about her plans for the Atlantic crossing.

"She knew more about aircraft and airways than any other person of her time, and in her death at such a youthful age, the world lost a genius who might have long since safely landed a space ship on the moon."

"There are no new worlds to conquer this side of the moon."

AMELIA EARHART, 1934

Introducing Amelia Earhart, a speaker once said of her:

I present to you evidence against a "lost generation," for I remind you that no generation which could produce Amelia Earhart can be called a lost generation. She has set a pace for those of her age and her time . . .

The New York Herald Tribune, 1934
(Women in the Changing World Conference, New York City)

Although praise and accolades were heaped upon Amelia from all quarters, Occasionally she was lambasted for some of her beliefs, opinions, and accomplishments. Fortunately, she was impervious to such attacks. In an editorial in *Airwoman,* February 1935, Mr. Swanee Taylor refers to an anti-Amelia editorial directed at her just after she became the first person to fly solo from Hawaii to Oakland, California:

Perhaps you heard the rumblings of that bilious piece called, "Amelia Earhart: A Flier In Sugar," appearing in the January 30th issue of none other than *The Nation?* This last one—just a few pot shots at the lady—came from the facile pen, if we are to believe a chaste footnote in that estimable magazine, ". . . a well known author . . ." who elected to blaze away from the comfortable ambush of a pseudonym.

Amelia Earhart after solo flight across the Atlantic in the Lockheed Vega, honored by a ticker-tape parade, New York City, 1932.

Amelia in the first Link Trainer in the Southwest, installed in Paul Mantz' United Air Services hangar at Burbank, where she practiced "blind" flying in preparation for her world flight.

COURTESY: DON DWIGGINS, FROM HOLLYWOOD PILOT, DOUBLEDAY & CO., 1967

1937 FIRST WORLD FLIGHT ATTEMPT

The flight was successful on the first leg, Oakland to Honolulu but on the second phase of the flight—Honolulu to Howland Island—a tire blew on takeoff. Paul Mantz, technical adviser sent the following message to A.E.'s husband George Putnam: "Amelia in crackup while attempting to take-off. Tire blew out. One wheel off. Propellers badly damaged. Oil dripping on runway. No one hurt. Amelia calm collected."

(*Berkeley Gazette*, March 20, 1937)

The flight was delayed until the plane could be repaired, which required that it be taken back to the mainland for repairs.

"I do not think 'blind' is an apt term for the type of flying meant. Instrument flying is not much better, for that makes it appear pilots use instruments only under certain conditions, when the fact is all modern flying is instrument flying. I prefer 'zero visibility,' or 'non-horizon' as opposed to horizon or which is generally termed normal flying."

AMELIA EARHART

A. E. in her "Flying Laboratory," the Lockheed Electra, examining a map. COURTESY: PERDUE UNIVERSITY

Amelia Earhart in front of the Lockheed Electra. Circa 1937. This photograph was used as the model for the U.S. Commemorative Stan

onor, 1963. COURTESY: LOCKHEED AIRCRAFT CORPORATION

In January of 1937 I flew to California. Circling Union Air Terminal at Burbank I landed, taxiing toward Paul Mantz' hangar, to see A.E.'s twin-engine Lockheed. I could just see the top of her head as she leaned forward in the cockpit. Pushing on the brakes and opening the throttle of my Beechcraft, I pulled up with a thunderous roar wing-to-wing with the "Flying Laboratory."

"Hey!" I yelled. No answer. "Ship ahoy" I called even louder as the engine sputtered into quiet death.

Peering through the small window, she squinted in my direction. "Would you please give me your autograph Miss Earhart?" I shrieked. "Hi,—get out of there," she yelled, legging out of the cockpit.

Halfway to my Beechcraft she was besieged, "Miss Earhart, would you mind giving me your autograph?" "Miss Earhart, I hate to bother you but would you sign this book for my little girl?"

Scrambling out of the ship I waited, standing on first one foot, then another, as Amelia with her usual graciousness signed—and signed.

"It must be wonderful to be famous," I leaned over to whisper. She giggled, that embarrassed little giggle which was part of her. "I'll fix you" she whispered back; then, aloud to the multitude: "You know Louise Thaden don't you? You should have her autograph." So I was in for it.

Her public taken care of, we walked arm-in-arm into the sanctuary of the hangar.

LOUISE THADEN

Louise Thaden, on her farewell to Amelia before her last flight:

In silence we walked to the car. "You know all the things I'd like to say," I said. Tanned hand on the door handle, blonde sunburned hair blowing in an off-shore breeze, she turned toward me.

"If I *should* pop off," she said, "it will be doing the thing I've always wanted most to do. Being a fatalist yourself you know The Man with the little black book has a date marked down for all of us—when our work here is finished."

Nodding, I held out my hand. "Goodby, and all the luck in the world!"

Perhaps it is because I have known Amelia for so long that I find it difficult to draw a word picture of her. Perhaps that is why it is impossible adequately to describe her staunch fineness, her clear-eyed honesty, her unbiased fairness, the undefeated spirit, the calm resourcefulness, her splendid mentality, the nervous reserve which has carried her through exhausting flights and more exhausting lecture tours.

As many another, I have often speculated on death and life hereafter. Eternal life, I think, is a life so lived that its deeds carry on through the ages. A.E. has carved a niche too deep to ever be forgotten. She will live. So I have said no farewell to her. As she invariably ended letters to me, so I say to her, "Cheerio!"

Louise Thaden in
High, Wide and Frightened, 1938

*A. E. with Marshall Headle (left) and
Paul Mantz. Circa 1937.*
COURTESY: LOCKHEED AIRCRAFT CORPORATION

*Harry Manning, A. E., Fred Noonan,
and Paul Mantz aboard the* Lurline
*after the first lap of their initial world
flight attempt nearest the equator,
1937.*
COURTESY: ATCHISON HISTORICAL SOCIETY

*Paul Mantz, A. E., Fred Noonan, and
Harry Manning in Hawaii.*
COURTESY: ATCHISON HISTORICAL SOCIETY

A. E. in Hawaii.

THE LAST FLIGHT June, 1937

Taking off from Miami, Florida, Amelia Earhart, Pilot, and Fred Noonan, Navigator, flew the *Flying Laboratory* Electra to French West Africa; then onward to India, Siam, and New Guinea.

Departing from Port Darwin on July 1st, they headed for Howland Island, 2,556 miles away. The next day weak messages were heard. The Electra, over Pacific waters with no land in sight, had only a half-hour's supply of fuel remaining. The last words radioed by Amelia Earhart were "Position doubtful."

> *Many a night I saw the Pleiades*
> *Rising through the mellow shade,*
> *Glitter like a swarm of fireflies,*
> *Tangled in a silver braid.*
>
> ALFRED LORD TENNYSON

Electra was one of the seven daughters of Atlas, and the so-called "lost" star of the Pleiades. It was in the Lockheed *Electra* that Amelia was lost. Alfred Lord Tennyson was one of Amelia's favorite poets.

Amelia Earhart and W. C. Tinus discussing the Western Electric radio equipment installed in her "Flying Laboratory."

COURTESY: BELL TELEPHONE LABORATORIES, INC.

38

WINGS OVER THE WATER

A tall girl, with a brave smile and tawny, tousled hair has gone to join the gallant group of men who have gone down to the sea in ships, and the ghostly gathering in Heaven's hangar will welcome her as one of their clan.

They will look up, those sailors of the skies who have flown and fallen, but they will not rise as a lovely lady enters. They will treat her like a man, like one of themselves, for that's the way she would have it.

In life she denounced the difference between men and women. She wanted an equal chance in the air, the right to fly wing to wing with other pilots, to go where they went, take the risk that they took, and if necessary, to die as they died.

RICHARDS VIDMER

"Wings Over the Water" is from a larger tribute to A.E. which appeared in Richard Vidmer's column DOWN IN FRONT.

A Kansas newspaper, the *Wichita Eagle,* ran an article in the July 25, 1963 issue, stating that the silver wings given to Amelia by the 381st Observation Squadron in 1929 were worn by Amelia on every flight except her last.

Is it merely coincidence that Amelia's grandfather was named Alfred *Gideon* Otis? Or that it was off *Howland Island* that Amelia Earhart and Fred Noonan went down July 2nd, 1937?

From a letter by John Dunning, dated July 12, 1983, author of *Tune in Yesterday, the Ultimate Encyclopedia of Old-Time Radio, 1925–1976*

"Amelia was to have been a special guest on the LUX RADIO THEATRE on her return from the world flight. The night she was to have been on, Cecil B. DeMille informed the audience that she was lost in the Pacific but that hope was still high for her survival. If I remember correctly, DeMille kept this up for several weeks, though his optimism obviously dampened quite a bit after that first week."

John Dunning, radio broadcaster and writer, Denver, Colorado.

Amelia in front of Lockheed Electra, with arms outstretched as if to embrace the whole world. COURTESY: LOCKHEED AIRCRAFT CORPORATION

Hail brother sailor, whither bound?
What is the course you steer?
Life's various perils press you round,
Dangers and death are near.

Now come about with steady helm,
Thy compass eye with care;
Thy pole-star watch in heaven's realm,
With faith and humble prayer.

Truth's light keep on the starboard bow,
Which shines so bright and even;
The spirit's breeze is blowing now,
Fair for the port of heaven.

Anon

South Wall Cenotaph, Seamen's Bethel,
New Bedford, Massachusetts

Next to Amelia's High School photo, Hyde Park,
Illinois, yearbook, the prophetic:

*"She sailed out of the dock
of nowhere into the sea of time,
bound for the port of nowhere."*

This untitled anonymous poem is inscribed on a South Wall
Cenotaph erected by the officers and crew of the *Gideon
Howland* as a token of respect to Simeon N. Bates, of Sandwich,
Massachusetts, 1st Officer of the ship, who died July 18, 1939,
AE 34, and Warren Wilbur of New Bedford, who died August
14, 1839, AE 21.

A. E. poses with her plane. COURTESY: HISTORY DIVISION, LOS ANGELES COUNTY MUSEUM OF NATURAL HISTORY

Coda

The official search by the United States Navy for Amelia Earhart and Fred Noonan was concluded on July 18, 1937. On January 5, 1939, in a Los Angeles courtroom, Amelia Mary Earhart was legally declared dead. (*Los Angeles Examiner,* January 6, 1939.) Fred Noonan had already been declared so. The other immediate crew members who had figured in the first world flight attempt nearest the equator have also passed on—Paul Mantz in 1965, and Admiral Harry Manning in 1974.

In the July 14, 1962 *Navy Times,* an article by Macon Reed, Jr., regarding joint rescue procedures, states, "In future air-sea rescue cases, all dates should be given in Greenwich Mean Time. The lessons and the mistakes of this flight and this search became the basis of much of the procedure in air-sea rescues that have saved many lives since then, and are still evolving toward more effective measures." Mr. Reed further states that "Miss Earhart flew to advance the interests of aviation. That was her mission. She may not have advanced them on this last flight in the manner in which she had envisioned, but advance them she did. However she came down, she was not a failure."

Searches still continue to this day in the far reaches of the Pacific for the physical remains of Amelia Earhart and Fred Noonan, and the Lockheed Electra plane which had carried the crew successfully three-quarters of the way around the globe nearest the equator.

When Amelia Earhart was declared lost at sea near Howland Island in the Pacific in 1937, people from all walks of life sang out their heartfelt grief at the loss of their "Mercury." The writer/poet H.I. Phillips, in his poem "Sun Dial," penned these lines to her:

Intrepid blazer of new skyway trails
No tragedy can dim your brilliant star,
No blow of fate can crush your well-won fame. . .

H.J. PHILLIPS

What though she went a-travel
Down paths you do not know?
Your words will not unravel
Webs that allured her so.

ARTHUR DAVISON FICKE

THE PEARLS

In this portrait by Ben Pinchot, Amelia is wearing her pearls, along with her wings of Honorary Major, 381st Air Corps Observation Squadron (now 381st Strategic Missile Wing. McConnell Air Force Base).

A. E. on Donrud Ranch, Wyoming, 1934. Photograph by Charles Belden. COURTESY: COLLECTION, CARL DONRUD

Whereas The Pilot section of this tribute centers on Amelia's contributions to Aviation, here in The Pearls emerge the lesser known facets of Amelia Earhart. Jewels of infinite variety reveal a feminine, graceful, funny, and multi-talented woman, beautiful in stature and in spirit.

Few are aware, for example, that Amelia was a talented fashion designer. Her designs sold in the Amelia Shop at R.H. Macy's in New York, and appeared in issues of *Vogue, Harper's Bazaar, Vanity Fair,* and *Woman's Home Companion.* In three consecutive years she was named one of the best dressed women, one of the world's most interesting women and one of America's twelve great woman leaders during the past hundred years, a tribute to her beauty and intelligence. Amelia's affectionate nature shines brightly in her letters to friends, several of which are included.

What's more, she was adept at photography, and enjoyed music, dancing, and sports. She danced with the Prince of Wales after the solo flight across the Atlantic. She attended the Olympics in Los Angeles in 1932, where she was photographed with Douglas Fairbanks and Jane Wyatt, and cheered Babe Didrickson (Zaharias) on to victory. Her ready wit and sense of humor proved an asset in both her writing and her public speaking engagements. In her writings, she combined the practical with the aesthetic. Sadly, many of her papers, or "peppers," as she called them, were burned in a fire at the Putnams' Rye, New York home, but some survive and appear here.

Amelia's review of Francis Walton's book, *Women in the Air* (Fararr and Rinehart) appeared in *The New York Herald Tribune,* November 17, 1935. And, from 1929 to 1930, she served as Aviation Editor for *Cosmopolitan* Magazine.

French literature and poetry appealed to her nature. She often translated into English poems that she loved, and was planning an Anthology of Poetry in which she would include her favorite poems.

Fond of the theater, Amelia was among the playgoers who saw "As Thousands Cheer," a satirical review written by George Kaufman and Moss Hart, with music by Irving Berlin. She also attended "The Good Hope," by Dutch playright Herman Heijerman—a drama about the sea that starred Eva LeGallienne. In addition, she wrote a review of the play, "Ceiling Zero," for *Stage.*

So, here then is the woman *beyond* the idolized heroine of aviation—the flesh-and-blood Amelia Earhart.

Photograph of Amelia Earhart for "Vanity Fair," November 1931, by Edward Steichen. COURTESY: MUSEUM OF MODERN ART

The Woman

A beautiful woman inside and out, Amelia Earhart possessed a femininity and a grace that came packaged with a sharp wit and droll sense of fun. A committed person, progressive in her thinking, and spirited where causes dear to her heart were concerned, there was also a softness to her. Affectionate in nature, she took the time to let her friends and family know it.

Amelia concerned herself with helping women achieve, not only in aviation but in other areas.

Her gift for bringing people together was evidenced in 1929, when she helped found the Ninety-Nines, an organization of women pilots named after the number of its charter members. Amelia was its first President. Today the Ninety-Nines is an international organization with more than 6,400 members in 33 countries around the world.

In retrospect it is easier to see how progressive Amelia Earhart was with respect to her thinking and her actions. I venture to say that she would have made a fine candidate for President of the United States, an Ambassador, or Secretary of State. Honest in her dealings with people, she was highly intelligent, high-minded, responsible, and caring.

A. E., Paris, 1932. COURTESY: ATCHISON HISTORICAL SOCIETY

48

A RECOLLECTION

BY LOWELL THOMAS

I was one of the lucky fellows who knew Amelia Earhart before my friend George Palmer Putnam talked her into marrying him. She was an exciting gal. I particularly admired her because she was feminine, beautiful, and always seemed to be master of every situation. Long, long ago I had the pleasure of presiding at an extraordinary party one evening, which was attended only by early Trans-Atlantic fliers.

Here is the list of those who were with us that evening:

Lon Yancey, Charles Lindbergh, Frank Courtney, Armand Lotti, Harry O'Connor, Bernt Balchen, Clarence Chamberlain, Dr. James Kimball, Ruth Elder, Peter Brady, James Fitzmaurice, and L.T.

Even in such company she stood out. All of the others seemed to regard her with some special affection.

If a girl was to fly across the Atlantic alone and so, in a sense represent America before the world, how nice it is that such a person is Miss Earhart. She is poised, well bred, lovely to look at and so intelligent and sincere.

MRS. HERBERT HOOVER

"Amelia was tall and straight and moved with incredible grace whether she was in long slim slacks or a floor-length dinner dress."

HELEN SCHLEMAN
Dean of Women, retired
Purdue University

This compliment has even more impact when one realizes that it was considered neither acceptable nor attractive in the 1930's for women to wear slacks.

In 1934, Amelia was chosen by the American Fashion Designers as the smartest dresser in aviation. Among others who made the list were Ina Claire, best dressed actress on the stage, and Mrs. John Hay Whitney, best attired sportswoman. In an Associated Press article entitled "Stylists Pick Queens; Mrs. Roosevelt One," Mary Elizabeth Plummer wrote:

"The critical eye of American fashion designers surveyed the style scene today and selected the country's best-dressed women."

Amelia in a long evening gown, speaking before a huge audience in Memorial Hall during her hometown welcome, 1935. COURTESY: ATCHISON HISTORICAL SOCIETY

Part of Amelia's magic was complexity, with an appeal for everyone. Her pants and short touseled hair belied her unexpected femininity, her exquisite hands, her directness of thought, her engrossing, poetic way with words. . . . She was a romanticist . . . "Dancing," she declared, "is the most wonderful pastime in the world."

FAY GILLIS WELLS
Charter-Member,
Ninety-Nines

In 1935, in a United Press copyrighted article, social leader Elsa Maxwell revealed her list of "The World's Ten Most Interesting Women." Amelia was among them. Others named were Marlene Dietrich and French writer, Collette. Said Miss Maxwell: "Fascination is an elusive quality that is fast disappearing . . . it is hard to find because is has nothing to do with beauty, charm, glamour, riches, or blueblood—only one woman in a thousand has it. Amelia Earhart has everything that fascinates."

TWO IMPRESSIONS OF AMELIA EARHART

BY ALICE KALOUSDIAN

(Impression One)

The long, empty stage is waiting for Amelia Earhart. The white screen in the rear has two doors to its right and left. They are primly closed. A wide arm-chair stands near one end of the stage. At 8:16 the door to the right is quietly opened, and Amelia Earhart appears.

She is a tall, slender lady who moves graciously and slowly. Her soft, winged jacket and tiny yellow curls suggest a bronze Mercury suddenly come to life. With a direct and simple smile of greeting she seats herself in the wide arm-chair and listens to the presiding gentleman as he speaks of courage and friendliness and of her. Not for a moment has she the air of one who is being talked about and looked at. She listens, instead, like a spectator of her own career. Her very long fingers move from the arms of her chair to her lap. Part of the record of the flight is in her fingers, I think, for they are at once artistically beautiful and full of motion and energy. I am admiring them when she rises to speak.

A. E. in her garden, Rye, New York. Circa 1933. COURTESY:
U.S. INFORMATION SERVICE, STILL PICTURE NO. 306-NT-279C-12, NATIONAL ARCHIVES

When the lecture is over, the audience leaves the theatre through one door and goes back stage through another. There is a large group of people waiting to meet Miss Earhart. For, according to some law of compensation, she who has been so alone in the air is surrounded by crowds the moment she touches earth.

I watch the audience as it files past the tall, gracious aviatrix. She greets everyone with kindness and simplicity. She smiles at the children, shakes hands with the ladies who thought she was charming, and promises her signature to the sandy-haired youth who feels he must have it. To the very professional young lady in black who asks journalistic questions and writes down the answers with an important-looking pencil, she is coolly polite. There is nothing in the tilt of her head, or in the warm glow of her eyes that suggests the much interviewed, photographed, and "autographed" personality. Fame and kindness are so little seen together, that it is beautiful and comforting to watch her who has them both.

We get a last glimpse of her as she enters the car that is to take her home. Her tiny, golden curls look powdery and regal in the light of the street-lamp. For a moment she looks at us with quiet, thinking eyes—then she is gone.

Though hers was a type of daring which was long thought to be a masculine derivative, Amelia Earhart was wholly feminine. One remembers the outward symbols of what she was—the slender hands and wrists, the fingers like an artist's, not strong enough, one would have said, to handle a great machine in the air; the voice that was soft and beautiful; the rich inflections, the animation that would have made the actress; the feminine dignity that melted into humor; the serious traits that made her effective as a social worker and a teacher; what she did, she did as a woman, in a womanly way, whether it was to receive with graciousness the public tributes she had earned, or to battle with storms above a dangerous ocean . . ."

ROBERT L. DUFFUS

However, the ancient and dogeared theory that the shape of the hands and fingers indicates talent or breeding can't be applied to modern hands. Amelia Earhart's hands give no indication of her work. They are long, rangy, and sensitive; perfect drawing-room hands that look altogether at home among fragile tea-cups and orchids despite the fact that they have guided a plane along thousands of miles over the turbulent Atlantic. She keeps them exquisitely groomed although she has never had a professional manicure.

DORIS LEE ASHLEY
(Excerpt) "By Their Hands You Shall Know Them"
Pictorial Review, October 1933

ADVICE TO AMELIA

Amelia Earhart is speeding across the Pacific on her round-the-world flight. She will have long boresome hours with little to do and much to think about. If we could catch her radio we would have just this one message, about as follows: "Amelia, dear, we knew your pappy when he was an amiable, carefree cake-eater in the University of Kansas, fifty years ago. So we have a right to take you aside and tell you something. It is this—we hope to heaven when you were packing your grip you put in a pocket comb. For you certainly need to comb your hair. Now is the time to get the tangles out and give it a good straightening. Your father had that tousled head and it didn't do him any good. He was obviously good-looking with it. So in the long lone watches over the gray and melancholy ocean, comb your head, kid, comb your head!

WILLIAM ALLEN WHITE

The hands of Amelia Earhart. COURTESY: NATIONAL AIR AND SPACE MUSEUM, SMITHSONIAN INSTITUTION, WASHINGTON, D.C.

WILL TELLS OF PLAYING HOST TO A FEW NOTABLES

BY WILL ROGERS
August 4, 1935

This Amelia, she would be great in any business, or in no business at all. She captivates the women too, which is unusual. She told me a lot about her trip to Mexico. She is crazy about Mexico . . . She sure has got nerve that gal . . . The thing I like about her is that she always has a fine word to say about all the other aviators. Not a one you mention but that has some particular quality or ability that she will boast as being superior to others. Jealously is not eating her heart out in regard to her fellow fliers, either male or female.

This is a portion of the last column Will Rogers wrote before his fatal flight with Wiley Post, August 15, 1935, Point Barrows, Alaska.

Will Rogers seated at his Remington typewriter.

COURTESY: WILL ROGERS MEMORIAL, CLAREMORE, OKLAHOMA

RADIO BROADCAST of February 3, 1935, from Carnegie Hall, New York City. WABC

Will Rogers introducing Amelia:
I got a great treat for you tonight. I got somebody here I want you to meet. You know, because we've heard so much about her lately, and I saw her come in the house tonight, and I said—"I'm going to get hold of you." And she said, don't you get hold of me, 'cause I don't want to get up here before the microphone," but I'm going to make her do it anyhow, and it's—and it ain't anybody but my friend and your friend, and my hero, and your heroess, and everything. . . . . . Amelia Earhart! Amelia come here. (applause)

Amelia was chosen as one of America's Twelve Great Woman Leaders During the Past Hundred Years by the women of America, along with Jane Adams, Founder of Hull House; Clara Barton, Founder of the Red Cross, and Harriet Beecher Stowe, Author.

An inspiration to women as well as children, Amelia received the eminent Achievement Award from the American Women's Association for her contributions to the Aviation industry. The award was presented to Amelia by Dr. Lillian Gilbreth, world-famous industrial engineer and management consultant, and mother of twelve children.

In 1933, A. E. was among the prominent women who, in a resolution, urged Soviet recognition of women. She also championed the cause for Helen Richey, the first woman airline pilot who would not be just a "fair weather" flier.

AMELIA, ON WOMEN:

"If enough of us keep trying, we'll get someplace."

Charter members of the Ninety-Nines, Inc., Amelia Earhart and Blanche Noyes, Mission Inn, Riverside, California, 1936.

This from her late friend, Blanche Noyes, Chief of the Federal Air Markings Program that sprang from Amelia's idea (see Pearls of Wit; Pearls of Wisdom):

> *"I believe Amelia did more than any other to encourage women in all careers. I will always remember her as the most human and humane person I have ever known."*

In 1935, Amelia Earhart accepted an appointment at Purdue University as Consultant in the Department for Study of Careers for Women, and served as Technical Advisor to the Department of Aeronautics.

ELEANOR ROOSEVELT ON AMELIA:

> *"She helped the cause of women by giving them a feeling there was nothing they could not do."*

Amelia and her camera, Carapito, Venezuela, June 2, 1937.
COURTESY: PURDUE UNIVERSITY LIBRARIES—SPECIAL COLLECTIONS

"Having lived a peripatetic life—never longer than four years in one place, with frequently lengthy excursions away from that, I suppose pictures mean more to me than to some people. They are stabilizers on a shifting world, and tend to keep records straight and memories fresh."

AMELIA EARHART
"Part of the Fun of It,"
(an article which appeared in
Vanity Fair, April 1933)

"I tried photographing ordinary objects to get unusual effects, and made a number of studies of such things as the lowly garbage can, for instance . . ."

AMELIA EARHART
Fun of It, 1932

PHOTOGRAPHY:

Amelia attempted commercial photography after taking a course in the subject through the University of Southern California. This was one of the ways she supported herself during the period of time that she was taking flying lessons from her first flying instructor, Neta Snook Southern. Amelia's studio was a short distance away from her home on Olive Street, in Los Angeles, California. She kept a darkroom notebook in which she recorded the necessary equipment she would need for her photography work and also added brief notes regarding composition and portraiture. Several of her own aerial and ground photographs appeared with the article she wrote, "Part of the Fun of It," which also advertised the Kodak Movie Camera Cine-K—April 1933, *Vanity Fair.*

MUSIC:

Amelia was actively fond of all kinds of music. She and her family took delight in attending concerts together. At Ogontz College (now a part of Pennsylvania State University), Amelia was recruited as a member of the mandolin society. Later, during her Columbia University days, she spent many hours listening to concerts on the steps in the gallery of Carnegie Hall.

A. E.'s sister, Muriel Earhart Morrissey, remembers that Amelia played the banjo for fun and taught herself to play the piano—sprightly tunes such as "Humoresque" and music by composers such as Mendelssohn. She was, in Muriel's words, "amazingly clever in learning to play any compositions she liked."

On concerts sponsored by the Department of Music, Drake University, Des Moines, Iowa, Muriel comments:

"For several years we had season subscriptions for the series, which included performances by some of the great artists of those days: Amelita Galli-Gurci, Marcella Sembrich, Madam Ernestine Schumann-Heink, Fritz Kriesler, Alma Gluck, and Rosa Ponselle."

MURIEL E. MORRISSEY
Courage is the Price

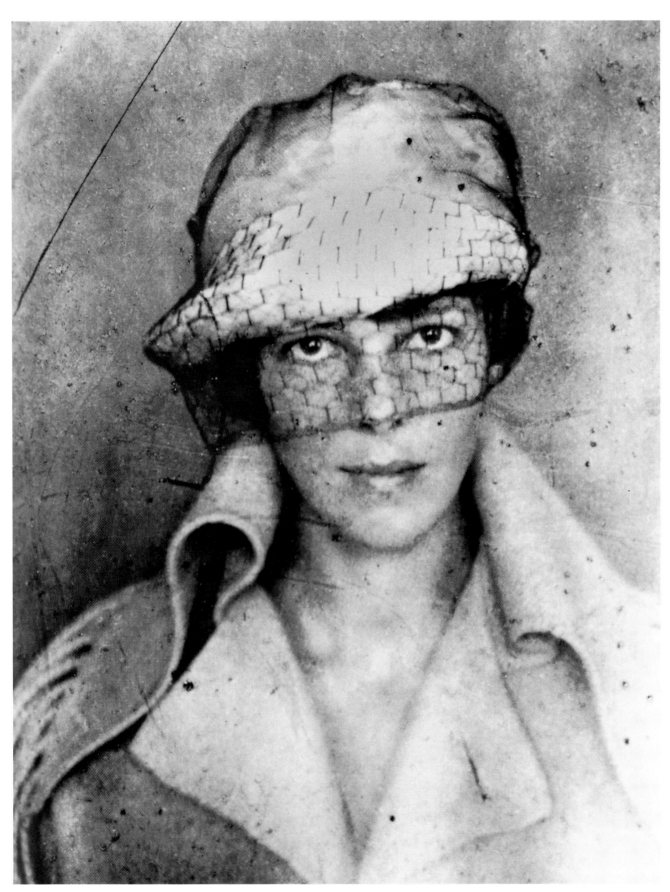

Only known self portrait of Amelia Earhart. COURTESY: JEAN L. BACHUS

Fashion Design:

Amelia had a gift for designing clothes that combined both the practical and aesthetic needs of the wearer. But this didn't come about overnight. Her sister, Muriel, recalls that even in their high school days, Amelia would make over some of their clothes, adding a different collar here or a ribbon there. One memory that stands out in her mind is Amelia taking some flowered curtain material that their mother had and making it into a most unusual tunic. Muriel had never before, nor has she since, seen such a colorful and tasteful combination as the floral pattern of that tunic against the dark green of the skirt with which it was worn. Another, recounted in *Courage is the Price*, is included here.

It was late in 1933 that her designs made their debut. In the December 11th, 1933, issue of *Woman's Wear Daily*, it was noted that Amelia Earhart would design some clothes, selecting her own materials and ideas. She created models for outdoor, travel, sports, and spectator wear.

Assisting Miss Earhart in marketing her designs countrywide was the R. H. Macy Company. In their advertisement in the January 1934 issue of *Harper's Bazaar* it was said of her:

> "To the intricacies of actual designing she brought two refreshing, almost surprising, abilities: unerring good taste, and a brilliant ingenuity of valid ideas."

In *Courage is the Price*, Muriel recounts the time Amelia made Easter outfits for them both from old silk pongee draperies after their father's hospital bills depleted funds set aside for that purpose. She writes:

> "You may not know it now, Pidge," she (Amelia) announced in mock solemnity, "but those beautiful Earhart girls are wearing the latest thing in pongee dresses for the Easter parade."
>
> "Neither Amelia nor I liked to sew. We knew nothing about the mysteries of cutting material from a pattern, but Amelia had an observant eye and an unusual sense of style. I was sent to buy green dye, matching grosgrain ribbon, and thread for my 'outfit.' Dark brown dye, ribbon, and thread were Amelia's choice. I tended to the dye department,

A. E. and her sister, Muriel. Utica, New York. Circa 1928.
CREDIT: SCHLESINGER LIBRARY, RADCLIFFE COLLEGE

> boiling, stirring, drying, and then trying again until, at last, the colors of the piece matched. Amelia drew her designs and then cut out a pattern from newspaper. Fortunately, the style for skirts was simple. It was the era of the much riduculed 'hobble skirt.' Amelia was an unorthodox seamstress, for she simply sewed two lengths of the dyed material together, gathered one end on a narrow belt, and turned the other end up so it cleared the floor eleven inches all around. Shoulder straps were attached to the skirt with large pearl buttons from Mother's wondrous button box. Ribbon bows at my neck and at my wrists disguised a white waist I had worn for more than a year. Amelia's skirt was the same, but she made herself a short sleeveless bolero jacket to wear over her renovated white blouse. A ten-cent bottle of 'hat lacquer' did wonders for our faded straws. I had a rosette of ribbon on mine while Amelia dyed a feather from our turkey-wing duster, and stuck it jauntily in the turned-up brim of her hat, in the style of T. R.'s Rough Riders.
>
> "As I left the house early Easter morning to sing in the choir, Amelia called from her window, 'If it should rain, for heaven's sake take off your hat and get under shelter or you'll leave a trail of green dye on the sidewalk.'"

Amelia wearing one of her own designs. Circa 1934–1935. COURTESY: NATIONAL AIR AND SPACE MUSEUM, SMITHSONIAN INSTITUTION

In the August 1934 issue of *Woman's Home Companion,* an article entitled "Designed By Amelia Earhart" was accompanied by a photograph of the designer, taken by Frederick Bradley, in which Amelia is wearing a suit with French cuffs (a favorite with her). The writer comments:

> *"We may not pilot a plane . . . but we do lead active lives, nearly all of us. And so she [Amelia] has set herself the task of designing clothes to fit—simple comfortable clothes, free of all the extraneous hangings even in the evening . . ."*

Amelia's thinking on ladies shirts with tails? Most practical. Said Amelia:

> *"I made up my mind that if the wearer of the shirts I designed took time out for any reason to stand on their heads, there would be enough shirt still to stay tucked in!"*

Amelia in the study of her Rye, New York home. She and husband George Palmer Putnam shared a love of good books, fine art and interesting people. COURTESY: LIBRARY OF CONGRESS

58

COURAGE

Courage is the price which life exacts for granting peace.
The soul that knows it not, knows no release from little things;

Knows not the livid loneliness of fear
Nor mountain heights, where bitter joy can hear
The sound of wings.

How can life grant us boon of living, compensate
For dull gray ugliness and pregnant hate
Unless we dare

The soul's dominion? Each time we make a choice we pay
With courage to behold resistless day
And count it fair.

AMELIA EARHART

Amelia wrote her famous poem while she was a social worker at
Denison House in Boston. The poem most probably appeared in
print for the first time in *Survey Graphic*, July 1928, shortly after
the *Friendship* Flight.

COURAGE

Point de paix sans courage, c'est de la vie le tribut exige,
L'ame qui l'ignore jamais n'est liberee des petitesses;

Elle ne connait ni la peur, sa solitude bleme.
Ni les sommets ou se goute l'amere joie
Du brussement des ailes.

Comment la vie pourrait-elle nous combler, compenser
La laideur grise et terne et la haine gravide
Si nous n'osions

Maitriser notre ame? A chaque fois que nous optons, nous payons
En courage le droit de voir le jour dans son eblouissement
Ainsi sommes-nous quittes.

AMELIA ERHART/1937
Tranduit de l'anglais par
Marie-Josephe de Beauregard
President Fondateur de la
Federation de Pilotes
Europeennes
Septembre 1983

A. E. at Mission Inn, Riverside, California. Circa 1936. CREDIT: SCHLESINGER LIBRARY, RADCLIFFE COLLEGE

A CHILD'S TRILOGY

These yellow things I love to see:
Clean, scrubbed lemons in the market stalls,
Our black cat's eyes at night,
And my bright new painted kiddie car.

Sometimes when I'm in bed at night
Lots of "I wonders" come to me:
Where does the fragrance of narcissus go
After the flowers fade?
Who cuts out the snowflakes from the big white
    clouds?
And is my lost jack-knife really in the moon?

AMELIA EARHART

This poem was probably inspired by children's remarks on the playground or in the game rooms of Denison House where Amelia was a social worker (Muriel Earhart Morrissey, *Courage Is the Price*). Yellow was one of Amelia's favorite colors. Both her car and her first airplane were bright yellow.

A CRITIQUE:
"CONCERNING KING LEAR'S MADNESS"

In the opening of the play, King Lear displays the unreasoning impetuosity and rashness of an unevenly balanced temperament. Social position has only augmented his natural vindictiveness, and so we can see him as a selfcentered old man with petty weaknesses. If we do not look at Lear in this light but assume his madness at the beginning, we lose half of the tragic nature of the drama. How much more potent is the effect of his raving in the storm when we consider it as the terrible consequences of Goneril's and Ragan's actions . . . "You heavens, give that patience, patience I need," and "I will be the pattern of all patience," just show his mutual anxiety which did result in his insanity, tho might not have.

AMELIA EARHART
Ogontz College notebook, 1916

In addition to writing her own poetry and prose, Amelia loved the writings of others, sometimes even translating her favorites into English. In February, 1920, while sitting on the library steps of Columbia University, she translated Paul Fort's charming verse. Here is the original in French, along with Amelia's painstaking translation.

HORIZON

Du cote de Paris, main vers Nemours la blanche,
un bouvreuil ce matin a chante dans les branches.
    Du cote d'Orleans, vers Nemours envolee, au coeur
du jour l'alouette a chante sur les bles.
    Du cote de la Flandre, au crepuscule d'or, loin de
Nemours la pie a cache son tresor.
    Le soir, criant vers l'est, l'Allemagne et la Russie, la
troupe des corbeaux quitta ce pays-ci.
    Mais dans mon beau jardin par Nemours abrite,
toute la nuit d'etoiles, Philomeme a chante!

PAUL FORT

On the way to Paris, toward Nemours the white,
a bullfinch in the branches sang through the morning light.
    On the way to Orleans, to Nemours flying feet, a swallow in the heart of day sang above the wheat.
    On the way to Flanders, in twilight's gold and gray, far from Nemours the magpie its treasures hid away.
    Eastward on to Germany and Russia with harsh cry, far away from this land, the crows of evening fly.
    But in my lovely garden, in Nemours' sheltered vale, all through the starry hours of night chants the nightingale.

TRANSLATION BY AMELIA EARHART

This poem, from the old *Literary Digest*, was one that Amelia selected for possible inclusion in the Anthology of Poetry she was planning to have published one day.

RESTLESS

I get tired of the same old house
And the same four walls.
I grow weary of familiar halls
And of clodding down known stairs.

I like to change my quarters now and then.
I like to change my aspect and my clothes
And feel foreign to myself
And hard for friends to recognize.

But if you will inquire for my soul
You will find it
Always at the same address.

ROBERT J. ROE

Laura Ingalls, Wiley Post, and A. E. having lunch at United Airport Terminal, Burbank, California, 1935.
COURTESY: ARCHIVES, DIVISION OF LIBRARY RESOURCES, OKLAHOMA HISTORICAL SOCIETY

WHAT ARE YEARS?
(3rd Stanza)

So he who strongly feels,
behaves. The very bird,
    grows taller as he sings, steels
his form straight up. Though he is captive,
    his mighty singing
says, satisfaction is a lowly
thing, how pure a thing is joy.
    This is mortality,
    this is eternity.

MARIANNE MOORE

This portion of Marianne Moore's poem so well fits with A.E.'s own philosophy that it could have been written with her in mind. In response to a letter of mine, in which I asked if she had ever met Miss Earhart, Marianne Moore replied: ''. . . admired her ability and courage; never met her, mourn in spirit whenever I think of her. . . . Quote me if you like.''

In this memorial piece, dedicated to his friend and partner Juan De La Cierva (1895–1936), Harold Pitcairn could well have been writing about Amelia Earhart. It was obvious to all who knew and loved her that she was extraordinarily gifted and, more importantly, that she reached out to share her gifts with others.

''It may be said, as it was said of old,
that others have labored and we have
entered into the fruits of their labor.
And it may be said that no man has died
too soon who has given the world a work
of genius and an example and inspiration
to all who may carry on his labors when
he is gone.''

HAROLD PITCAIRN

Juan De La Cierva was the inventor of the Autogiro (forerunner of the helicopter). It was in a PCA-2 Autogiro that Amelia set the first official rotary-wing altitude record.

62

FRIENDSHIP:

Amelia's affectionate nature is captured both in this letter to Orville Wright, and in her tribute to Wiley Post:

August 6, 1932

My dear Mr. Wright:

The other day I had the fun of cracking a bottle of gasoline on the nose of a new automobile. I am just dropping this line to tell you that my fun was increased when I found that the one I christened was for you. I think the Terraplane is a great little car, and I hope my naming yours will add to your pleasure.

I wish that it were possible for your many friends in the East and West to see you more often. Perhaps the new Essex will help us to do so!

Sincerely yours,

AMELIA EARHART

(From the Orville and Wilbur Wright Papers, Manuscript Division, Library of Congress, Washington, D.C.)

WILEY POST

I used to know Wiley Post. I met him first when he was a test pilot for Lockheed in 1929 and I had just bought my number one Vega for the women's air derby.

Six years is a long time for pilots doing the kind of flying Wiley did to know each other. But through our period of acquaintanceship he changed not a whit. No demonstrations, no public acclaim affected his simplicity or sincerity of purpose. Perhaps in addition to his willingness to share with others anything he found out about planes or motors, his most dominant characteristic was his complete unconsciousness that what he did had any value or color. So close was he to his profession that he could not see the sheen on his own wings . . .

Wiley Post is gone. Pioneering to the last, three hundred miles within the Artic Circle! Lost to the world are his ability, his humor, his conquering spirit. Lost to his friends are his tales of adventure, told while he denied he had any.

AMELIA EARHART

(An excerpt from Amelia's essay that appeared in the October 1935 issue of *Forum and Century*.)

A. E., Wiley Post. Union Terminal, Burbank, California. Photograph by J. H. Washburn.

COURTESY: LOCKHEED AIRCRAFT CORPORATION

Robert Browing, a favorite poet of the Earhart family, penned these words; they exemplify Amelia's feelings on friendship.

Hand grasps at hand, eye lights eye
in good friendship, and great hearts expand and grow
one in the sense of this world's life.

ROBERT BROWNING
FROM ''SAUL''

Pearls of Wit;
Pearls of Wisdom

Amelia Earhart possessed a thoughtful, quiet wisdom beyond her years, particularly evident here in her words on war and on art. She respected both the written and spoken word, but this respect went hand-in-hand with a sense of fun and a delightfully droll way of making words get up and dance. Here, for your enjoyment, then . . .

ON PHOTOGRAPHY:

I tried photographing ordinary objects to get unusual effects, and made a number of studies of such things as the lowly garbage can, for instance, sitting contentedly by its cellar steps, or the garbage can alone on the curb left battered by a cruel collector, or the garbage can, well—I can't name all the moods of which a garbage can is capable.

AMELIA EARHART
Joy Hopping and Other Things,
Fun of It, 1932

ON SHARING THE LIMELIGHT:

I have been congratulated for swimming the English Channel, and being picked up by a ship near the Azores. So I received a few inquiries meant either for Gertrude Ederle or Ruth Elder. I have always felt that the three of us were somewhat thoughtless to have names all beginning with E.

AMELIA EARHART
Fun of It, 1932

ON HER COLUMBIA UNIVERSITY DAYS:

The steps in the gallery of Carnegie Hall are really not uncomfortable and I enjoyed many a concert from that locality—after I got used to the smell of garlic.

AMELIA EARHART
Fun of It, 1932

ON THE ATTRIBUTES OF HER "YELLOW PERIL:"

My roadster was a cheerful canary color . . . It had been modest enough in California, but was a little outspoken for Boston, I found.

A.E.

Amelia's 1922 Kissel "Goldbug," nicknamed "The Yellow Peril," is included in the collection of the Forney Historic Transportation Museum, Fort Collins, Colorado.

ON HER EXPERIENCES AS VICE PRESIDENT OF THE NEW YORK, PHILADELPHIA AND WASHINGTON AIRWAYS:

On the line, we carried some express and odd packages of all kinds. I, myself, chaperoned a canary from New York to Washington. The bird appeared much more frightened in the air than some of the other animals that patronized us! One of these was a pony. For some reason or other, there was a rush about getting him from Philadelphia to the Capitol. So he was sold two seats (although he had to stand partly in the aisle) and made the voyage very comfortably. To prove he really flew, he had his picture taken wearing a pair of goggles as he alighted.

AMELIA EARHART
Fun of It, 1932

Amelia Earhart possessed a sense of humor that stayed with her under the worst conditions. It is particularly evident here, in her letter to Eleanor Roosevelt after having been the butt of some unpleasant press:

50 West 45th Street,
New York City.
March 14, 1935.

Dear Mrs. Roosevelt:

"Wall, I sure am glad to be here, and gosh, I sure do hope I'll meet the Prince of Wales" was the quotation attributed to me in 1928 after the Friendship flight. It happened I said not *one single word* on the subject and the whole was fabricated out of one reporter's imagination. I can laugh at it now. I only hope some day I can laugh also at the preposterous "starvation interview" the press has had me give concerning my stay at The White House. . .

Something I said (I can't think just what yet) must have been misinterpreted and passed round by word of mouth, since more than a week elapsed before it got into print.

I am humiliated that any incident should have occurred to mar what was so delightful an interlude. It's an ill wind that blows nobody good. Perhaps you *will* let me raid the ice-box sometime, not because it's necessary but because it's fun.

Humbly and devotedly yours,

Amelia Earhart

Landing in Newark, New Jersey, after historic solo flight from Mexico City.

ON THE DANGERS INVOLVED AFTER LANDING:
(After her history-making solo flight from Mexico City to Newark, New Jersey, 1935).

In due course I was rescued from my plane by husky policemen one of whom in the ensuing melee took possession of my right arm and another of my left leg. Their plan was to get me to the shelter of a near-by police car, but with the best of intentions their execution lacked coordination. For the arm-holder started to go one way while he who clasped my leg set out in the opposite direction. The result provided the victim with a fleeting taste of the torture of the rack. But at that, it was fine to be home again.

A.E.

Both her fondness for friends, and her impish sense of fun shine through in this droll letter to Harry Manning, who was to have been her navigator on the first attempt to circumnavigate the world at the equator in 1937. However when the second leg of the flight had to be rescheduled, time constraints prevented his participation.

Harry Manning (1897-1974) was one of the few holders of the Gold Congressional Life Saving Medal of Honor, received in 1929, along with a New York ticker-tape parade. He had personally directed the lifeboat that negotiated gale-slashed Atlantic seas to rescue the entire 32-man crew of the stricken Italian freighter *Florida*.

After he was graduated from New York Nautical School (now the U.S. Merchant Marine Academy), his

67

Harry Manning and Amelia Earhart, 1937. COURTESY: JONNI EISENHARDT

February 19, 1934

expertise as a navigator accelerated his rise through the ranks. In 1928, by the age of 32, he had his first command, the S.S. *President Roosevelt*. It was while he was commander of this ship that he first met Amelia.

He served as advisor to the United States Lines during the construction of the super liner at Newport News, and was named Master of the 900-foot, 53,000-ton ship when it was put into service in 1952. On her maiden voyage, Manning was in command when the *United States* broke the Queen Mary's 14-year-old record for the west-to-east Atlantic crossing from Ambrose Light to Le Havre, France. On its return trip, the *United States* broke the Queen Mary's east-to-west record, and brought America its first laurels and trophy in this competition in 100 years! Manning, and his Chief Engineer, William Kaiser, rode in the lead car up Broadway in Manning's second ticker-tape parade. He was promoted to Vice-Admiral in 1971 "in recognition of a distinguished service in the maritime service."

Dear Harry:

To take almost a year in answering a letter is about my average rate just now. My friends suffer most, because I am continually shoving their letters aside telling myself they will understand delay while a business correspondent will not. I know my theory is unjust, for I value friends more than I do the butcher, baker or candlestick maker, worthy souls though they may be. What to do about regulating my life and letters, I know not. . .

What are you doing besides being on the *California?* I know that doesn't fill all your time, unless you've changed. Books, music, etc. still interest you, I hope.

I have found a number of people in my journeys who know you. I can't tell you who they are, but they seem to be ubiquitous. Possibly being a ship's officer—an attractive one—is one of the best means of acquiring a large circle of friends.

Write me at Rye, or here at the Seymour.

Sincerely yours,

Amelia Earhart

A. E. at her home in California. Circa 1934. CREDIT: SCHLESINGER LIBRARY, RADCLIFFE COLLEGE

ON THE BEAUTY OF NATURE:

From her essay on *Clouds,* this portrait of clouds. . .

". . .Dawn touches them with rose which melts to gold; evening colors them with myriad changing tone until gray envelopes all. . ."

A.E.

From *Soaring Wings,* by George Palmer Putnam, this on shadows:

"The sun comes up to put shadows into the world— dark definite ones. No one has seen a tree who has not seen it with its shadow, from the air."

A.E.

From *Last Flight,* this:

". . .from the air . . . of whatever country, ever changing, ever shifting in coloring, light and shadow hold beauty which only the willfully blind could ignore."

A.E.

MORE ON SHADOWS:
From her Columbia school days:

I have sat in the lap of the gilded statue which decorates the library steps, and I was probably the most frequent visitor on the top of the library dome. I mean the top.

I used my knowledge of how to get on the dome a few years later when I was again at Columbia. It proved an excellent vantage point for watching the eclipse of the sun in 1925. I stood there with a well-known biologist and looked across at the angel trumpeting on the highest point of St. John's Cathedral. We three appeared to have a better view of the galloping moon shadows than anyone else in the world.

AMELIA EARHART
Fun of It, 1932

ON GOD:

Asked her idea of God by Alice Denton Jennings in an interview for the *Atlanta Journal,* Amelia responded unhesitatingly: "I think of God as a symbol for good, identifying good in everybody and everything. This God I think of is not an abstraction, but a vitalizing, universal force, eternally present, and at all times available."

ON WAR:

Amelia was a pacifist. She spoke out on many occasions on the subject. And in an interview for *The Yale Daily News* of November 10, 1933, she is quoted as saying:

Women should be drafted . . . I think very likely this would tend to discourage war, it would make two nations lining up on the battlefield even more ludicrous than they are now. Also I believe the oldest people should be drafted first. They are the ones who start war, and if they knew their verdict to fight meant their getting out in the line of fire themselves, they would be a great deal slower in rushing into armed conflict.

AMELIA EARHART

Earlier, in 1916, Amelia wrote: I realized what the World War meant. Instead of new uniforms and brass bands, I saw only the results of a four years' desperate struggle; men without arms and legs, men who were paralyzed and men who were blind.

A.E.

ON ART:

Art appeals to us not for anything, whether color, tone, form or movement, in the work itself, but for the value of something elsewhere suggested by the work of art. Art is significant, i.e., it has life-giving power. This life-giving power is conveyed through tactile values and movements.

AMELIA EARHART
Ogontz College notebook, 1916

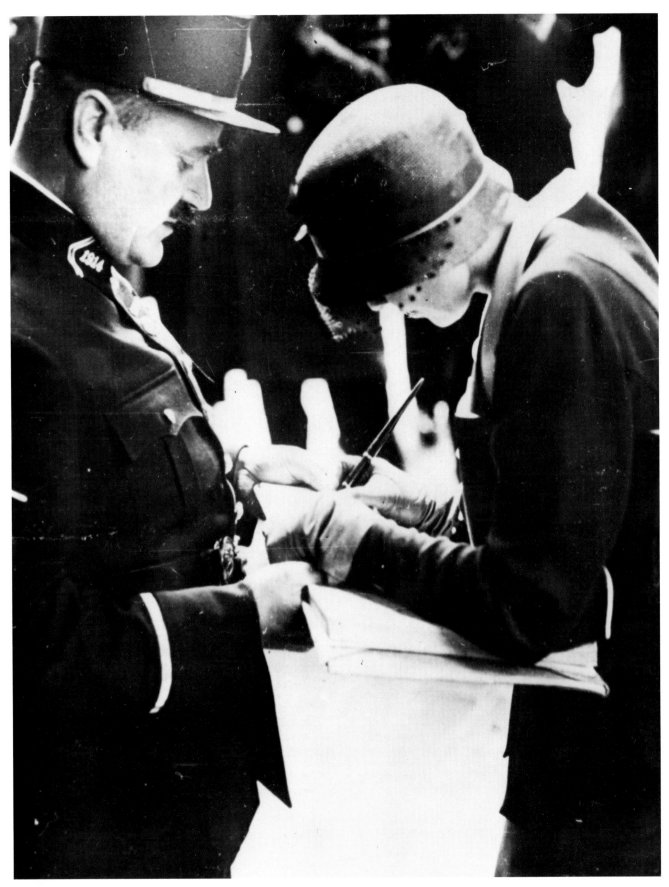

Amelia Earhart, signing the register, Tomb of the Unknown Soldier, "Eternal Flame," Paris. COURTESY: SMITHSONIAN INSTITUTION

On Aviation as Portrayed by Hollywood:

"Amelia Earhart Looks at the Films"

An exclusive interview with Mortimer Franklin for *Screenland* Magazine:

Do I think the motion pictures have made the most of the dramatic possibilities that aviation holds?" She considered the question a moment, her frank, pleasant features made pleasanter still by a ready smile as replete with warmth as it is devoid of affectation.

"No, I don't think they have. But that," she added quickly, "is speaking only from the viewpoint of a practical flyer. I'm not going to pass judgment on dramatic values from the standpoint of the motion picture, because it's a thing I don't know about."

"Certainly I feel," she continued thoughtfully, "that there is a great deal of color, human interest and suspense in flying which the films have yet to discover. . . . I think it's too bad when aviation movies depend for their excitement upon plane wrecks, lost flyers, and all that sort of thing. Perhaps that's good drama, perhaps it isn't; but it certainly isn't modern aviation. It's an unfortunate point of view, though understandable enough, that producers sometimes adopt toward pictures: they feel that they must drag in a few crack-ups to provide thrills."

Interviewer Mortimer Franklin responded with:

For all Miss Earhart's diffidence regarding knowledge of dramatic value, she has come perilously close to proclaiming an important truth to which producers might well pay heed . . . Great drama concerns itself with the conflict of men's souls and their destinies. It is such conflict rather than 'thrill' drama that the aviation films have yet to show us.

On Navigation Aids:

And oh, for a country-wide campaign of sign painting! Coming down through a hole in the clouds, any flyer is thankful for definite information as to his location, even if it is only to check his navigation. . .

There is another side to this sign painting business. The city in which you live should be proud enough of itself to be recognized by air travelers. Often the thousands who pass by on the airways can't do so unless the name is prominently displayed. Though there has been much progress made in the past few years, there is many a community whose shingle might be hung out for the air traveler. Large white or chrome yellow letters painted on some flat roof should announce the names of all progressive cities and towns to the flying world.

AMELIA EARHART—1932

This idea resulted in the Federal Air Markings Program, which was carried forth in the beginning by pilots Phoebie Omlie, Louise Thaden, and Blanche Noyes. Ms. Noyes became Chief of the Program.

On the Future of Aviation:

I maintain my prophecy that aviation, as we know it today, will be accepted as an everyday means of locomotion before we progress to stratosphere flying.

AMELIA EARHART
from *Fun of It*, 1932

I would rather be on the side of those who believe anything possible, who have faith in man's skills in the wings he has found.

I am sure there are no unknown worlds left to conquer this side of the moon.

AMELIA EARHART

Miscellaneous Observations:

It usually works out that if one follows where an interest leads, the knowledge of contacts somehow or other will be found useful, sometime.

AMELIA EARHART
from *Soaring Wings* by George Palmer Putnam, 1939

. . .You will find the unexpected everywhere as you go through life. By adventuring about, you become accustomed to the unexpected. The unexpected then becomes what it really is—the inevitable.

AMELIA EARHART
from *Soaring Wings* by George Palmer Putnam, 1939

Amelia told her students at Purdue:

"Learn by doing, and have fun doing it. . ."

Amelia as Inspiration

A pioneer of aviation with an artist's view of life, Amelia Earhart's style, individuality, graceful wit, and sharp intelligence has held and stretched the imagination of countless artists engaged in every art form and medium. In the lightening dance of her life, she captured their interest, thus generating and unleashing a positive creative force which resulted in the representative pieces that appear here.

Her likeness has been drawn, painted, carved, sculpted, and etched. Cameras have caught and preserved the depth of her beauty—both physical and spiritual. And, she's been praised in song, in poetry, in prose, and in dance.

An inspiration during her lifetime; today, fifty years later, she is an inspiration still. . . .

In the words of President Dwight David Eisenhower, who was himself a pilot:

> *"Miss Earhart opened new areas to the view and vision of her fellow citizens. Her soaring spirit continues to lead the way to endless opportunities of life."*

Amelia Earhart. Oil on canvas 3' × 5'. Howard Chandler Christy, American illustrator and painter, 1897 1952.

EXHIBITION: 1937, THE WILLIAM ROCKHILL NELSON GALLERY OF ART, ATKINS MUSEUM OF FINE ART, KANSAS CITY.

AMELIA EARHART

She could not keep her feet upon the ground,
So lightly poised she was, tiptoed and questing
Like a winged Mercury; and all the round
Circumference of the sky had known her breasting
Of sleet and wind, the lightening and the rain,
Less clamorous to her, intrepid rover,
Than feverish shops and droves of huddled men
Who fight for room to breathe till breathing's over.
And when some Heavenly Hunter shot her down
The blue abyss of sea could little smother
That free rebellious spirit which had known
Three Elements already—now Another
Has claimed her soul of unimprisoned rapture
Which three alone could never wholly capture.

RALPH MORTIMER JONES

We ask not how she fares, who in the skies,
On earth-fledged wings spanned continents and seas,
And sought as all Icarians must, to rise
Into white beams of beckoning mysteries.
Though prone to ease, and by stale custom tamed,
Still we remember her, nor shall forget,
For in our thoughts she lives. Her courage flamed,
And its immortal, steadfast flow has yet
The power to set some brooding heart agleam,
Stir from its shroud some splendid dusty dream.

FRANCES ALICE WARD

Lovely bronzed lady with the tousled hair—
Stand on the farthest silver tip of your dear plane
And look them in the face—these craven men—
As even Christ looked searching eyes at other men
    When Mary sought his arms.
They say you flew for fame—you of all girls,
    Who'd flown the seven seas,
They say you flew without a purpose to pursue—
You with new instruments testing both wind and
    space.
You flew, my dear, straight to the world of God—
There were no routes you had not charted here.
And when you looked at death, her sable skirts
    All fringed with light,
I know you said, with starlight in your eyes,
'Dear God, what fools men are to fear this loveliness!'

DUDLEY FIELD MALONE

FOR AMELIA EARHART

We shall forever think of you with wings,
And courage quite indomitable, and gay.
We may forget such dear and intimate things
As tousled hair, and laughter, and the way
You waved from cockpits, and the times we said
You so resembled Lindbergh, or he you,
And even this: with what concern we read
That you were lost somewhere beyond the blue.

But there will be the thought of wings above
Both land and water when your name is spoken
(Spoken with kindly reverence and love),—
And there will be this heritage: unbroken
And beautiful courageousness you gave
Us who have much to learn of being brave.

ELAINE V. EMANS

ONE FROM NINETY-NINE

Is life more truly ours than yours,
Loved friend we toast tonight?
Are you less present here than we
Who share the candlelight?
Must life be certified in years
And memory by authentic tears,
Or may we hail with valiant cheers
The living . . . not in sight?

Bright spirit of the blue frontier
Where silver navies ply,
No place on all this rolling sphere
Can claim that there you lie.
Though wind and tide may have your wing
They cannot quench that living thing,
That deathless passion which must sing
Its song against the sky.

GILL ROBB WILSON

Drawing of Amelia Earhart in profile. James Montgomery Flagg.
COURTESY: FAITH FLAGG, THE ARTIST'S DAUGHTER

Strandenaes at work in his studio, New York City. Oil on canvas, 33½" wide × 59½" high. Amelia Earhart in flying togs, 1928. Original painting was presented by George Palmer Putnam, 1939, Purdue University (Earhart Hall), West Lafayette, Indiana. COURTESY: NATIONAL AIR AND SPACE MUSEUM, SMITHSONIAN INSTITUTION

Nimble Feet Trip Earhart Hop

Aviation 'Motif' One Of Many When Terpsichore Shuffles Sectional Dance Favorites

FLIGHT OF THE PLANE

ALTITUDE

SPIN

The EARHART HOP

HAPPY LANDING

Aviation has put its imprint on the dancing art, as these sketches showing some of the steps in the new Earhart hop reveal.

*Milton Caniff's lively drawing of the "Earhart Hop."
Danced to the Foxtrot rhythm, the Hop was demonstrated by Lucille Stoddart and Lawrence Hostetler during the Dancing Teachers' Congress held in July, 1932, at the Hotel New Yorker, New York City. Amelia once said, "Dancing is the most beautiful pastime in the world."*
COURTESY: MILTON CANIFF

Robert York's drawing, in tribute to Amelia Earhart, June 12, 1937. COURTESY: THE LOUISVILLE TIMES

That Amelia was a vehicle through which other women lived vicariously is epitomized in this poem:

(Written June 17, 1937, just after the start of A.E.'s second attempt, World Flight).

Ask not of your confreres—ask not of the flyers—
Ask not of lesser birdmen who master the wheel;
Feel the lurch and the lift and the spinning depth,
Only to circle an arc of the skies of home
And drop to the landing field—ask not of the sparrow
With wings but not the will to precede you or follow,
Eagle, what it is that you seek and find.

But ask of the bound, O free one. We can tell you—
We the girls at the desks, knowing the sky
A square between rocking buildings, we the girls
Making the motion over and over again,
Straightening the back for a respite, seeing the sky
Grimed by a smoky pane—bending forever
As a wheel turns and bends to its weight, without rest.

Or ask of us, caught by a slender thong
To the wrists of the men we love. Ask of the mothers
Sending the children to school, pacing the close rooms
Doing the same small tasks, hearing the door slam,
Handing out cookies, hearing the door slam again;
Whose men come home and wash and sit at dinner
Saying the same words over and over again,
Till the lights go out, and the dark is full of warmth
And whispers, and cries of babies yet born and unborn.
Ask of the falcon never freed to soar,
What it is you seek and find, O stormy petrel,
Out there with the wet on your wings, with the chill of
    night
On your eyeballs—skimming the swells of the seven
    seas.

You are the one who takes the wings of the morning
To the uttermost parts of the sea. You are the searcher,
The keen-eyed huntress, never the prisoned heart.
You are the Woman claiming the thing denied.
You are the free-foot boy on a windy upland
Alone with his dog while the sun hangs under the east.
And we who can never precede you nor follow know
What rare game you flush, and are with you in the
    capture,
Where steadfast from nose to tail your vibrant pointer
Startles and holds for all time the wild bird of dawn.

MARY FINETTE BARBER
Brooklyn Poet

SONIC MEDITATIONS:
TEACH YOURSELF TO FLY
(DEDICATED TO AMELIA EARHART)

Any number of persons sit in a circle facing the center. Illuminate the space with dim blue light. Begin by simply observing your own breathing. Always be an observer. Gradually allow your breathing to become audible. Then gradually introduce your voice. Allow your vocal cords to vibrate in any mode which occurs naturally. Allow the intensity to increase very slowly. Continue as long as possible naturally, and until all others are quiet, always observing your own breath cycle.

Variation: Translate voice to an instrument.

PAULINE OLIVEROS

SONIC MEDITATIONS is dedicated to the Women's Ensemble and Amelia Earhart.

"Miss Earhart's Arrival, Hanworth, 1932." Oil on canvas, 28¹/₈" high × 72¹/₈" wide. Walter Sickert, English Impressionist, 1860–1942. Exhibitions: London, 1932; Carnegie International Exhibition, Pittsburgh, 1933; "Late Sickert," Hayward Gallery, London, 1981–1982; Permanent Collection, The Tate Gallery, London.

THE MOTHER MEDITATES
(CONCERNING AMELIA)

Now as I wait through troubled days and nights
For you who gained renown—the world's acclaim,
Remembering your past successful flights,
Fearing, yet hoping this would be the same,
My grief-torn heart is proud of you, and yet
There have been times I almost wished that you
Had been more like the women who beget
A family - but you were of the few
Who have the spark that makes them ever go
Adventuring and seeking, never still…
And have you gained at last what you would know
And landed on some high, celestial hill?

MARGARET E. BRUNER

IMPRESSION

While we remember you, could we do other
Than tread with eager feet the toilsome road,
View with undimmed eye the wreck of cherished hopes,
And bear with dauntless heart rude buffetings of fate.

ROBERT A. WINSLOW, JR.

In process a kind of music occurs naturally. Its beauty is not through intention, but is intrinsically the effectiveness of its healing power.

PAULINE OLIVEROS

81

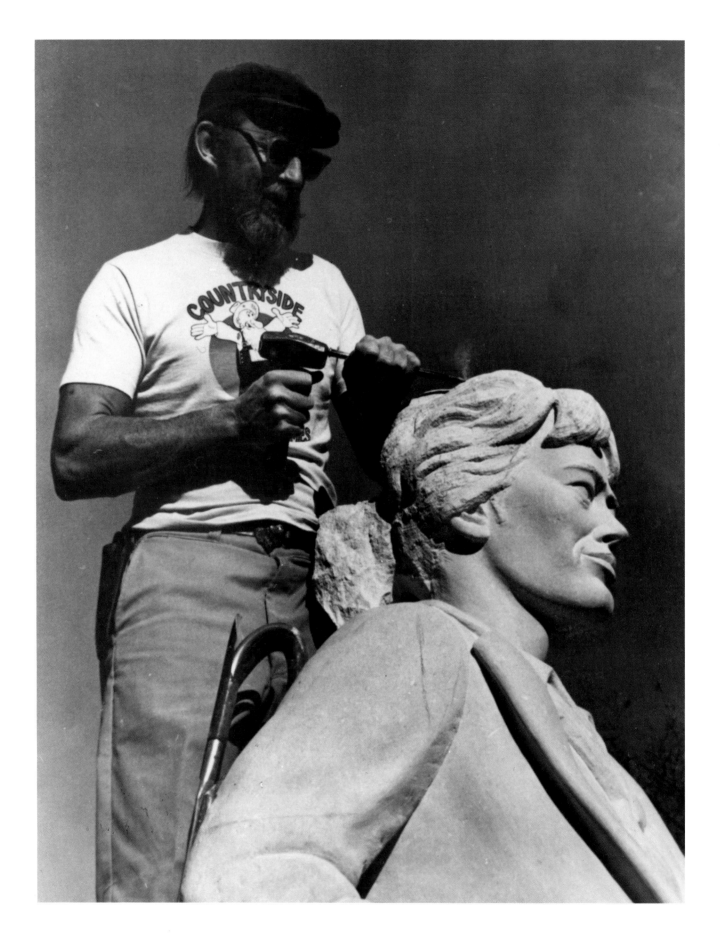

Sculpture of Amelia Earhart by Sally Clark. Exhibition: 1962, Graham Gallery, New York City. (In private collection.)

PHOTOGRAPH BY PETER A. JULEY AND SON, NEW YORK CITY.

Pete Felten at work in his studio. Silverdale stone sculpture of Amelia Earhart, one of a series of four entitled "Four Kansans." Exhibited in a niche at the State Capitol, Topeka, Kansas, 1981. PHOTOGRAPH BY CARLA KROELL.

If a star had translated her
We could have allowed her to a star;
If the lightening had claimed her
In a swift embrace, we
Could have afforded her to fire;
Had our Mother Earth enfolded
That chrysanthemum head,
Those flowering hands,
Only with tears should we have minded.

But she was not for the sea,
The lumbering, felonious,
Unflorescent sea,
Oh, never never for the sea.

Somewhere in a sounding cave
Of a silver shore she lies,
Where the running waters break
Morning and evening in a lily spray
Preserving her coral tomb.

And there the waves forever chant
Her symbolic name—
Amelia, Perseverance!
While the seagulls answer
That knew her realm:
Amelia, Amelia, Amelia!

Her name riming with America,
Hither in loving memory
Singing we bring her home—
'Amelia—America;
'America—Amelia.'

ALBERT EDWARD JOHNSON

About poets, A.E. Johnson remarked:

"Great poets never write from ivory towers. The Whitmans and Shakespeares come walking, and in jeans. Their message shames us by showing us a more excellent way of talking about life. Poetry is the conscience of the world."

Figure of Amelia Earhart by A. C. Ladd, 1937. This foot-high bronze was given to Thiel College, Greenville, Pennsylvania, by A.E. just a few months before her disappearance over the Pacific Ocean. COURTESY: THIEL COLLEGE ARCHIVES

David T. S. Jones working on clay stage of his life-size bronze statue of Amelia. Photograph by Sylvia Messick. COURTESY: ATCHISON HISTORICAL SOCIETY

84

"Pioneers in Progress," panel two. Wood sculpture by John Rood. Carved in Philippine and Honduran mahogany, 37¾" high × 8' wide × 3¾" thick. Exhibition: On permanent display at American Association of University Women National Headquarters, Education Center, Washington, D.C. Amelia Earhart, second figure from the right, appears along with Susan B. Anthony, suffragist; Sarah Josepha Hale, educator; Jane Adams, founder of Hull House; Mary Cassatt, Impressionist painter; Maude Adams, actress and theater innovator; Edna St. Vincent Millay, poet and dramatist; and Florence Rena Sabin, M.D. Of this effort, Rood said: "I wished to show the drive, energy, adaptability, resourcefulness, and patience which I feel are, in a large sense, attributes of women—all things eternal and basic. COURTESY: AMERICAN ASSOCIATION OF UNIVERSITY WOMEN

AUDE ADAMS + EDNA ST. VINCENT MILLAY + AMELIA EARHART + FLORENCE R. SABIN

IMPRESSION

Not in a little dust quiescent,
Nor stilled beneath the ocean's roar;
Her voice is in the night wind's sigh. .
More plaintive now the seabirds' cry. .
A wraith enchanted, beauty haunted;
Seeking, calling, evermore.

ROBERT A. WINSLOW, JR.

Poet Frieda de Garavito penned this tribute to Amelia in Spanish. Below is her translation into English, along with the Spanish version.

"POST MORTUM"
TO AMELIA EARHART

Too soon destiny took you away
Valiant aviator
With lillies of glory she
covered your breast
Laurels caress your blonde tresses
dressed in mourning
the sea carried you away
Our banner dedicates a hymn to you.

"POST MORTUM"
A AMELIA EARHART

Demasiado temprano el destino te llevó,
Aviadora, más valiente de esta era
Vestido de luto el mar te recogió
Con lirios de gloria tu pecho cubrió
Laureles acarician tu rubia cabellera
Un himno te dedica nuestra bandera.

Marble portrait bust of Amelia Earhart by
Brenda Putnam. COURTESY: DESMOND O'HARA. THE
ARTIST'S NEPHEW

Amelia Honored
and Immortalized

Over the years, Amelia Earhart has been installed, enshrined, decorated, honored, exhibited, and inducted. Many monuments—some of material, some living and breathing—have immortalized her. For example, Amelia, with her droll sense of humor, would be amused to learn that a Bald Eagle at the San Diego Zoo is named "Amelia" in her honor! Of her many honors, only a few have been selected for this volume.

Schools in Detroit, Chicago, Alameda, Wichita, and Hialeah bear her name. On the campus of Purdue University, residential halls Earhart East and Earhart West honor her. In Burry Port, Wales, a 6-foot monument, commemorating the Friendship Crew Crossing of 1928, still proudly stands in the town.

A residential hotel in Wiesbaden, Germany, honors her memory, as does a mountain peak in Yosemite National Park, named by the Rocketdyne Mountain Club. A tidewater dam that spans the Mystic River at Somerville, Massachusetts, bears her name.

GOLD MEDAL OF THE CITY OF NEW YORK:

Amelia Earhart being presented with the Special Gold Medal of the City of New York after her solo flight across the Atlantic. Mayor Jimmy Walker, A.E., and George F. Mand, Chairman of the Mayor's Reception Committee, 1932. COURTESY: ATCHISON HISTORICAL SOCIETY

Amelia Earhart was awarded the Gold Medal of the City of New York after her solo flight across the Atlantic in 1932. Mayor Jimmy Walker made the presentation.

Said Mayor Walker:

"You have contributed greatly to the science of aeronautics."

THE DISTINGUISHED FLYING CROSS:

On July 29, 1932, Amelia Earhart became the first woman to receive the Distinguished Flying Cross. She was decorated by the Vice President of the United States, Charles Curtis.

U.S. Vice President Charles Curtis from Kansas presenting the Distinguished Flying Cross awarded to Amelia Earhart by the U.S. Congress. Los Angeles, July 29, 1932. Governor James Rolph (right) looks on. Amelia was the first woman to receive the Distinguished Flying Cross.
CREDIT: ASSOCIATED PRESS. CLIPPING FROM ATCHISON GLOBE, *JULY 21, 1963*

SPECIAL GOLD MEDAL OF THE NATIONAL GEOGRAPHIC SOCIETY:

Amelia Earhart was the recipient of the Special Gold Medal of the National Geographic Society, in 1932. Presenting the medal was President Herbert Hoover.

Amelia Earhart receiving the Special Gold Medal of the National Geographic Society on June 21, 1932. Presenting the award in the Rose Garden at the White House is President Herbert Hoover. Looking on are Mrs. Hoover, Dr. Gilbert Grovesnor (President of the National Geographic Society), George Palmer Putnam, and Dr. John Oliver La Gorce (Vice-President of the Society). COURTESY: ©*NATIONAL GEOGRAPHIC SOCIETY*

The Society of Woman Geographers awarding its First Gold Medal to Amelia Earhart. Presented by President, Mrs. Harriet Chalmers Adams, at reception in New York, January 5th, 1933, held at the home of Mr. and Mrs. George Arents, Jr. COURTESY: COLLECTION OF THE SOCIETY OF WOMAN GEOGRAPHERS

SPECIAL GOLD MEDAL OF THE SOCIETY OF WOMAN GEOGRAPHERS:

In 1933, Amelia Earhart was awarded the first Gold Medal of the Society of Woman Geographers. Presentation was made by Mrs. Harriet Chalmers Adams, President, at a reception held at the New York home of Mr. and Mrs. George Arents, Jr.

THE COLUMBIA BROADCASTING SYSTEM MEDAL FOR DISTINGUISHED CONTRIBUTION TO RADIO ART:

When Amelia was presented with the Columbia Broadcasting System medal for distinguished contribution to the radio art, the ceremony was broadcast over the Columbia network. Henry Adams Bellows, Vice President of CBS, made the speech of presentation, and Miss Earhart's acceptance speech was also broadcast.

Mrs. E. F. Hutton presenting the Cross of Honor, U.S. Flag Association, to Amelia Earhart. June 20th, 1932, Bryant Park, New York City. COURTESY: HILLWOOD MUSEUM, WASHINGTON, D.C.

THE CROSS OF HONOR
OF THE U.S. FLAG ASSOCIATION:

Presentation of the Cross of Honor was part of our nation's welcome home to Amelia after her solo across the Atlantic. Colonel James A. Moss, Founder and President General of the United States Flag Association, was present at the impressive ceremonies in New York City. Mrs. E. F. Hutton made the presentation.

The Cross of Honor is engraved with these words:
FREEDOM—EQUALITY—JUSTICE—HUMANITY

Cross of Honor.

COURTESY: NATIONAL ARCHIVES, WASHINGTON, D.C.

97

INTERNATIONAL HONORS:

BELGIUM:
ORDER OF LEOPOLD
Presenter: King Albert (Brussels).

FRANCE:
CROSS OF LEGION D'HONNEUR
Presenter: Paul Painleve, Air Minister (Paris).

MEXICO:
ORDER OF AZTEC EAGLE (Posthumous Award)
Presenter: Renato Cantu Lara, Mexican Consul (Los Angeles).

ROMANIA:
VIRTUTEA AERONAUTIC
Presenter: Charles A. Davila, Romanian Minister to the United States (New York City).

UNITED STATES OF AMERICA:
THE DISTINGUISHED FLYING CROSS
Presenter: Vice-President Charles Curtis (Los Angeles).

NATIONAL GEOGRAPHIC SOCIETY
SPECIAL GOLD MEDAL
Presenter: President Herbert Hoover
(Washington, D.C.).

HONORARY DEGREES:
Amelia would accept only two honorary degrees.

The first was from Thiel College, Greenville, Pennsylvania, from which her father, Edwin Stanton Earhart, had graduated. On December 11, 1932, Amelia accepted the Honorary Degree of Doctor of Science from this institution, and spoke on the theme "Beauty in All Fields of Work."

The Honorary Degree of Public Service was conferred upon Amelia Earhart on May 26, 1935, by Oglethorpe University, Atlanta, Georgia.

The citation read:

"The First Lady of American Skies, the Stormy Petrel of the Seven Seas, the Golden Plover of the highway of heaven."

The degree was presented to Amelia by the Honorable Eugene Talmadge, Governor of Georgia.

In 1936, Amelia was honored by the U.S. Naval Academy. Here are the details, extracted from the letter of tribute, dated 28 August 1968, from the Superintendent:

". . . Amelia Earhart was, of course, a distinguished pioneer in the field of aviation and her courage, consumate skill, dedication, and accomplishments in the field of transocean air navigation entitle her to the gratitude, appreciation and sincere respect of all Americans. . . .
. . . the Naval Academy paid tribute to Amelia Earhart in a somewhat unique fashion during her lifetime. On the invitation of Rear Admiral David Foote Sellers, Superintendent of the United States Naval Academy in 1936, Miss Earhart addressed the first class of the Brigade of Midshipmen. She was the first woman to address the Brigade or any part of it, since the Academy was founded in 1845."

JAMES CALVERT
Rear Admiral, U.S. Navy
Superintendent

WOMEN'S SPORTS FOUNDATION HALL OF FAME:

In 1980, Amelia Earhart (along with Gertrude Ederle, Althea Gibson, Eleanor Holm, Mildred "Babe" Didrikson Zaharias, and Patty Berg) was inducted into the Hall of Fame Pioneers, of the Women's Sports Foundation.

AMELIA EARHART MADE HONORARY MAJOR IN THE AIR FORCE:

Amelia received the honorary rank of Major in the United States Army Air Corps and was awarded her wings in 1929 by the commander of the 381st Observation Squadron.

In 1935, a Medal of Honor for Amelia Earhart was proposed by Representative John H. Tolan of California, and again in 1937, a bill proposing a Medal of Honor for Amelia Earhart was introduced into the House by Representative John H. Tolan to be given Amelia Earhart upon her return from her World Flight.

First day of issue, July 24th, 1963, Atchison, Kansas, Amelia's birthplace.

AMELIA IMMORTALIZED ON A U.S. COMMEMORATIVE STAMP:

During the A.E. Stamplift of 1962–1963, a battle of sorts ensued with the Post Office Department over their interpretation of "deep and lasting significance to the nation as a whole" (their yardstick for decision-making as to who will or will not be honored on a U.S. stamp).

Stamp crusader Gretchen Foy penned this argument in Amelia's favor:

> *Diogenes could seek her like,*
> *Held high his gleaming lamp,*
> *And few he'd find—yet bear in mind,*
> *There is no Earhart Stamp!!*

And, here is a portion of a letter to LIFE Magazine by Clara Studer, instigator of the concerted Stamplift Crusade:

LIFE Magazine: To the Stamp-inclined Editorial,

So O'Henry had to wait for the Russians to take note of his birth (shame on us Texans) in order that Sam Rayburn's dome, conjointly with that of the Capitol, might grace a postage stamp here. Just as *Amelia Earhart* was "by-passed" (The tactful P.O. word) in favor of the Battle of Shiloh, say, or the 150th Anniversary of the Louisiana Purchase . . . already honored philatelicly six times before! . . .

The spontaneous crusade of American Youth has borne fruit, with no campaign manager, press agent, funds or agenda! The Century of Progress of Women has been at a standstill as far as philatelic immortality is concerned since 1948, unless you count Betsy Ross showing the flag to three men, minutely, or Susan B. Anthony on a 50¢ non-commemorative. . . . Thousands of letters from individuals, organizations both national and local, have requested this one. Now the *National Council of Women*—sponsors of a list naming Amelia one of the twelve Great Women Leaders of the past century—has, through its Executive Director, Mrs. Edmund Haines, requested AN AMELIA EARHART AIRMAIL COMMEMORATIVE STAMP! . . . . Whereas Fannie Hurst writes: "I am pained and surprised at the failure of the Post Office Department to immediately recognize the validity of Philatelic honor for this key woman. AREN'T WE ALL! . . .

On April 25th, 1963, at the National Aviation Club, the unveiling of the design of the Amelia Earhart Commemorative Airmail Stamp took place. Then, on July 24th—Amelia's birthday—an international celebration was held in honor of the first day of issue. Held in her home town of Atchison, Kansas, the celebration was attended by the Postmaster General, along with many celebrities. The Ninety-Nines had their first international airlift that day, flying special first-day covers to all 50 state capitols by relay. Seven of the original charter members of the Ninety-Nines flew them from Kansas. From New York, the covers were flown to London, Paris, Rome, and Brussels, where champagne receptions were held at American Embassies.

AMELIA EARHART

THE ATLANTIC   HARBOR GRACE   TO IRELAND   MAY 1932

Maurice Heaton's glass mural of Amelia Earhart's flight across the Atlantic. PHOTOGRAPH: OLAF STUDIOS, NEW YORK CITY.

Maurice Heaton's glass mural, located in the New Roxy Theater in Rockefeller Center, New York City, remained there until the demise of the theater. Eugene Schoen, Interior Architect for the New Roxy theater, suggested the subject and the original concept of the design.

The mural portrays the flight of Amelia Earhart across the Atlantic. Vertical bands of red and mauve color suggest the side curtains of a stage, behind which is the sea and the sky. The sea is represented as alternating waves of blue and green broken arbitrarily, with the silhouette of New York at the left, and Ireland at the right. The sky is a simple series of horizontal bands, each receding over the next. In the middle of the mural

is the aeroplane, leaving behind it streamers of glistening transparent lines crossing a cloud formation in deep blue. In front of the aeroplane is a thunderstorm, treated as geometrical disturbances of the sky lines; the lightening and rain-drops are etched in transparence.

The mural is illumined from behind by electric reflectors and mirrors. The colors (vitreous glazes fused permanently on the glass at high temperature) diffuse and soften the light.

One feels in seeing the mural that the modern treatment of the subject is more the result demanded by the technique developed by this artist than the mere wish of the designer to be modern at any price.

EARHART LIGHT:

At Diamond Head, on the Island of Oahu, stands a stone memorial bearing a brass plaque inscribed "Amelia Earhart—First Person To Fly Alone From Hawaii To North America January 11, 1935." A Chinese Banyan tree marked with her name grows in the Grove of Celebrities, in Liliuokalani Park, Hilo. And farther out, beyond Hawaiian waters on Howland Island*, Earhart Light guides wayfarers to safety.

*Howland Island was named by Captain George E. Netcher in 1842, for he found on the island in the Pacific a seaman's grave identified by a monument as that of a member of the crew of the ship *Gideon Howland* of New Bedford, dated 1839. Even earlier, in 1830, Captain Daniel McKenzie, Master of the ship *Minerva Smyth* reported his discovery of the island.

In Chicago Illinois, Earhart Elementary School immortalized Amelia with their school song:

EARHART ELEMENTARY SCHOOL SONG

(Sung to the tune of "Daisy Bell"—popularly known as "On a Bicycle Built For Two." Words and music by Harry Daere 1892, T. B. Harms and Company, copyrighted 1892).

> Earhart, Earhart, better than all
>   the rest,
> Earhart, Earhart, able to pass
>   the test.
> We're loyal and always show it,
> We want you folks to know it,
>   And we are proud
>   To be part of the crowd
> Of the wonderful Earhart school.
>
> Earhart, Earhart, our colors are
>   blue and white;
> Earhart, Earhart, whose students
>   are very bright.
> Our P.T.A. is dandy,
> Their help is always handy.
>   Our teachers—great!
>   They really rate
> At the wonderful Earhart school.

SOME EARHART STREETS:

In Los Angeles, California, Will Rogers Street and Earhart Avenue intersect. This would have pleased both Will and Amelia. Will wrote of Amelia in his last column, and introduced her warmly when she appeared on his radio show. (Enjoy both Rogers-isms in "The Woman" section of this volume.)

In Newfoundland, in the town of Gander and on the western outskirts of St. John's, Earhart Street is joined by other streets named in honor of pioneer aviators such as Harry Hawker and McKenzie Grieve. Amelia, who encouraged women in all professions, would be pleased and gratified to know her street is near those named after two outstanding and courageous Newfoundland women:

ETHEL DICKENSON, a nurse in the 1918 flu epidemic, who lost her life helping others.

MARGOT DAVIES, a wartime broadcaster.

Both of these women showed courage "above and beyond." Amelia would have been proud of them.

SHRINE OF AVIATION, J. F. K. INTERNATIONAL AIRPORT, NEW YORK CITY:

The airplane models which hang there are votive offerings given by the various airlines in the same manner that sailors of old gave ship models to be hung in the churches of Europe. A different airline is remembered by name during each Sunday service.

Each December 17 a Solemn Eucharist in memoriam is held, at which the famous departed in the air industry are commemorated.

KATHERINE A. BRICK

On December 17th, 1976, Amelia Earhart was the first woman to be so honored. The model of the Lockheed Vega, in which she became the first woman to solo across the Atlantic, was consecrated.

Amelia's spirit of excellence continues in the scholarships of The Ninety-Nines International and Fellowship Awards given by Zonta International.

Astronaut Sally Ride, a Ninety-Nine, exemplifies this new generation of the pilot-scientist.

AT LOGAN INTERNATIONAL AIRPORT, BOSTON, MASSACHUSETTS, AMELIA'S NAME IS PRESERVED:

On July 25, 1963, a Northeast Airlines Jet Overhaul Center was dedicated in her name by members of the Ninety-Nines.

On March 1, 1984, the Amelia Earhart General Aviation Terminal, the first major aviation facility of its kind anywhere, was dedicated to her. The terminal sits on a landfill known as Bird Flats. This modern structure, with an atrium and a skylight, contains a Flight Operations Center, a conference room, and a pilot's room.

THOUGHTS UPON THE OCCASION OF THE DEDICATION OF A NEW SCHOOL

(Written for the dedication of the Amelia Earhart School in Alameda, California, on October 6, 1979).

A school is a wondrous place,
Whether it be old with Ivy-colored walls,
Worn steps, and scarred desks within,
Or new, with gleaming glass and steel
In handsome functional design . . .

Pride in his own good work of mind or hands
Is the precious heritage of every child . . .

In this fast-changing world, our youth must know
That integrity and faith alone change not . . .
Your elders salute you all, as you begin to tread
The torturous, yet often Joyful, path to life's maturity.

MURIEL EARHART MORRISSEY

BICENTENNIAL HYMN

I walked alone in the International Forest of Friendship today, and there was no sound in the world. I trod the white and curving paths in alternating sun and shadow as fickle as February clouds would trap and then release the sun. I stepped as though a sound might somehow waken all the sleeping trees that are not yet bedded in that fertile soil.

MICKEY PARMAN

INTERNATIONAL FOREST OF FRIENDSHIP:

The International Forest of Friendship was a gift to America from the international organization of women pilots—The Ninety-Nines—and from the City of Atchison, Kansas, birthplace of Amelia Earhart, the Ninety-Nines' first president. The gift was presented on America's 200th birthday in Amelia's name.

The Forest, overlooking Lake Warnock, is made up of trees from the 50 states, territories, and the 33 countries around the world where there are Ninety-Nines.

Winding through the forest is Memory Lane, tying America's flying past to its future, honoring those who have, or who still are, contributing to all facets of the advancement of aviation.

THE INTERNATIONAL FLIERS WALL, RIVERSIDE, CALIFORNIA:

Instituted by Frank Miller and dedicated in 1932, the Flier's Wall is the exterior south wall of the St. Francis Chapel, which is the International Shrine of Aviators. It is located in the Atrium of Mission Inn, Riverside, California.

Amelia Earhart's signed No. 20 copper wings were added on February 3, 1936.

The International Flier's Wall, Riverside, California. Instituted by Frank Miller and dedicated in 1932, the Flier's Wall is the exterior south wall of the St. Francis Chapel, which is the International Shrine of Aviators. It is located in the Atrium of Mission Inn, Riverside, California. Amelia Earhart's signed No. 20 copper wings were added on February 3, 1936.

Acknowledgments

A special thank you to Muriel Earhart Morrissey, in giving of her time, and allowing several unpublished writings by her sister Amelia to appear herein—critique on King Lear and an excerpt from her paper on Art; both writings done while attending Ogontz College.

And a very special thank you to Fay Gillis Wells, Charter Member of The Ninety-Nines, friend of Amelia's, in bringing the reality of Amelia's personality into focus, and in giving unstintingly of her time.

My gratitude to Captain Irene N. Wirtschafter, USN (Ret.), for her perceptiveness, interest, and loyalty to my project.

Of the many deserving my gratitude for their contributions to this volume, several must be mentioned: Father Angelus Lingenfelser, President, Atchison County Historical Society, Atchison, Kansas; Keith Dowden, Special Collections, Purdue University Libraries, Lafayette, Indiana; John Cahoon, History Divison, Natural History Museum of Los Angeles; and David Kuhner, The Norman F. Sprague Memorial Library, Claremont, California.

A thank you to Nancy Link Powars, who had faith in my project and brought it to fruition.

To the editor, Beverly Bohlinger Hegmann, and the designer, Gerard A. Valerio, who used their expertise to bring beauty and harmony to this book, my sincere gratitude.

To those persons visible and invisible who have helped to shape this tribute to this pioneer Woman of aviation and space—Amelia Earhart—a thank you.

And to those that trusted this neophyte author with their personal material. Thank you for that trust.

Biographical Profiles

(In alphabetical order)

MARY FINETTE BARBER (1898–1979)

Won the Columbia University Writers Club prize for the best short poem of 1926; won the prize again in 1930 for the best poem of that year. Her poetry has appeared in *Poetry World* and *Southwest Review*.

MARIE-JOSEPH de BEAUREGARD (Nee Galtier d'Auriac)

Family history is firmly planted in Gascogne. An international journalist, she has researched contributions of the development of women in aviation in France and the world. A volunteer with the French Forces, 1939–1945 (7th Army), Marie-Joseph was a member of the European Movement and of the International Liaison of Association of Women. She is a member of the Ninety-Nines as well as President-Founder of the Federation of European Women Pilots. Among her distinctions: Chevalier de la Legion d'Honneur and the Croix du Combattant (France et Liberation).

WILLIAM ROSE BENÉT (1886–1950)

Author of numerous volumes of poetry and verse. Recipient of many awards, including the 1942 Pulitzer Prize for Poetry. During his career as an editor, he worked on *Century* magazine, *The Nation's Business*, and *The Saturday Review of Literature*. Born in Fort Hamilton, New York, he received a Doctorate of Literature from Dickinson College, and was co-editor with Norman H. Pearson of *The Oxford Anthology of American Literature*, 1938.

KATHERINE A. BRICK

Driving force behind the votive model of Amelia Earhart's Lockheed Vega which hangs in the Chapel at John F. Kennedy International Airport, New York. Former WASP Squadron Commander and member of the Thunderbolt Pilots Association. Recipient Paul Tissandier Diploma, Federation Aeronautique International. Writer of many articles in various publications, including ''Amelia Earhart's Legacy'' for *U.S. Lady*.

ROBERT BROWNING (1812–1889)

English poet. Born at Camberwell. *Pauline*, a dramatic poem written at the age of nineteen, was published in 1833. Later works include: *Men and Women* (1855), *Bells and Pomegranates* (1841–46). His masterpiece, *The Ring and the Book* (1869), is an epic dealing searchingly with the passions of humanity.

MARGARET E. BRUNER (1886–1971)

Wrote a weekly column, ''In Thoughtful Mood,'' for the *News Republican* of Newcastle, Indiana. Her work has appeared in numerous anthologies, newspapers, and magazines.

MILTON CANIFF

Creator of ''Terry and the Pirates'' and ''Steve Canyon'' cartoons, began his career in 1921 with the Dayton, Ohio, *Journal Herald*. Named to the National Comic Strip Hall of Fame in 1981.

DUSTIN W. CARTER

A founding member of the American Aviation Historical Society, with membership No. 9, is Past President. Recently completed his second volume *Racing Planes and Air Races—A Biennial Covering 1976–1977 Air Races*.

MAY CHITTIM

Music teacher and Arranger. Born in Belle Fourche, South Dakota, she grew up in an isolated corner of northeastern Wyoming. During the Depression years she played piano for dances, adding to the family income. Later she started a family band, began writing her own orchestrations, and played on Sunday evenings for the United Service Organization (U.S.O.). Arranged A.J. Maurer's song ''Amelia, Queen of the Air.''

HOWARD CHANDLER CHRISTY (1873–1952)

Illustrator and portrait painter. Perhaps most remembered for his creation of the "Christy Girl." His works include "The Signing of the Constitution" in the Capitol, Washington, D.C.; "Signers of United Nations Charter," at San Francisco, and "Life of Thomas A. Edison," Capitol building, Columbus, Ohio. He maintained his studio at Des Artistes, in New York City.

SALLY CLARK (1883–1981)

At age 50, inspired by the work of her husband (a fine sculptor in his own right), Sally Clark began sculpting on her own. Her bronze statues can be seen at the American Museum of Natural History and the Explorers Club, New York City, as well as the Boston Museum.

FRIEDA de GARAVITO

Poet, New York City. Her poetry has appeared in published form. No other biographical information available.

ROBERT L. DUFFUS (1888–1972)

Reporter for the *San Francisco Bulletin*, 1911–1913. Also wrote for the *New York Globe*, and in 1937 became a member of *The New York Times* editorial board. Born in Waterbury, Vermont, he wrote a number of books including "The Arts In American Life" with Frederick Paul Keppel (1933), and "The Tower of Jewels" (1961) about his early days on the *San Francisco Bulletin*.

ELAINE V. EMANS

No biographical information available.

PETE FELTEN

Began sculpting at age 24. His recent works—Four Kansans, (Dwight David Eisenhower, William Allen White, Amelia Earhart, and Arthur Capper)—are in niches at the Kansas State Capitol in Topeka.

ARTHUR DAVISON FICKE (1883–1945)

Born in Davenport, Iowa. Graduated Yale University 1904; taught English at State University of Iowa until 1907. His well-known poetry compositions include "The Happy Princess" (1907), "Twelve Japanese Painters" (1913) and "Sonnets of a Portrait Painter" (1914).

JAMES MONTGOMERY FLAGG (1877–1960)

Born in Pelham Manor, New York. The style of James Montgomery Flagg was derived from the great pen-and-ink illustrators of the turn of the century. He is best remembered for changing Uncle Sam from a hayseed into a strong, dignified figure with his recruiting poster "I Want You."

PAUL FORT (1872–1960)

French poet and critic. In 1895 he began to publish lyrical and balladesque impressions; later collected in thirty-eight volumes, entitled *Ballades Francaise* (1897–1940 and 1946; *Selected Poems and Ballads of Paul Fort*, 1921).

ALICE ROGERS HAGER (1894–1969)

Correspondent and writer. Started as a reporter in Los Angeles, California. Free-lance reporter for the *Washington Star*, the *New York Times* and other publications. War correspondent, China-Burma-India theatre, 1944. Public Affairs officer (attaché), U.S. Embassy Brussels, Belgium 1948–1952. Among honors: Southern Cross (Brazil) and Order of Merit of Santos Dumont.

MARY HALPERIN

No biographical information available.

MAURICE HEATON

Born in Switzerland. A third-generation stained glass craftsman. In 1947, he invented a process of fusing crushed crystals of enamel to glass. Today he is recognized as the sole creator of a glass unique in texture and color. His work is in the permanent collections of the Metropolitan Museum of Art, New York City and the Corning Glass Museum, Corning, New York, and others. It has also been on exhibit across the United States and has been displayed in international ceramic and glass shows. An illustration of his glass appears in the *Encyclopaedia Britannica*.

ALBERT EDWARD JOHNSON (1890–1960)

Born in London, England, he began teaching poetry, drama and writing at Syracuse University, New York, in 1924. His poetry has been published on both sides of the Atlantic in *Swanee Review* and *Punch*, among others. His books include *The Crown and the Laurel*. He was an elected member of Japan's Poets Club in 1952, the fourth non-Japanese writer to receive such an honor.

ROBERT UNDERWOOD JOHNSON (1852–1937)

Originator of the Rome Memorial to Keats and Shelly; was Ambassador to Italy and in the forefront of the international copyright movement.

DAVID T.S. JONES

Instructed in pastel drawing by his mother; studied drawing and painting under Thomas Knowles, British painter and illustrator. Also studied music composition under William Kent, a student of Paul Hindemith, as well as sculpture under Robert Eberhard, a former student of Auguste Rodin.

RALPH MORTIMER JONES (1879–1969)

Minister, poet, writer, and an able cartoonist. Born in Wolfville, Nova Scotia. He was educated at Acadia College, (now University), and the Baptist Seminary in Rochester, New York. His published works include several children's poems, including "Bed-time" and "Oxen." His daughter recalls, "His mind seethed with wit and a quiet love of just being alive."

ALICE KALOUSDIAN

No biographical material available. Thought to have been a student at Hunter College, New York City, 1932. Wrote *Two Impressions of Amelia Earhart*, which appeared in the *Hunter College Echo* Christmas, 1932, and a poem, "To One I Know," which appeared in the same issue.

RICHARD LE GALLIENNE (1866–1947)

Wrote many books of poetry. His extraordinary poem, "The Second Crucifixion," is in *Robert Louis Stevenson and Other Poems*, and was recited by his daughter, Eva, on a recording of English and American Poetry on Theatre Masterworks. His book *Attitudes and Avowels,* from which "Clouds" was extracted, includes *The Human Need of Coney Island, On Airships and The Soul of Man,* and, for the writer, *The Word Business.*

HAROLD A. LEVEY (1894–1967)

A protegé of Victor Herbert, Mr. Levey conducted "The Only Girl" at age 19 on Broadway. His radio musical credits include "Theater Guild of the Air," "NBC Symphony," and "Cavalcade of America." He composed and conducted for Henry W. Savage, the Schuberts, and Florenz Ziegfeld. On television, Mr. Levey composed and conducted all original music for "Armstrong Circle Theatre." He played the classics and Tin Pan Alley tunes, swing and jazz, and conducted for vaudeville as well.

WALTER LIPPMANN (1889–1974)

A recipient of a Pulitzer Prize, as well as many honors; he strongly influenced American public opinion both in editing *The New York World* and in founding *The New Republic.*

DUDLEY FIELD MALONE (1882–1950)

An internationally known lawyer and poet, he served as counsel with Clarence Darrow. Assistant Secretary of State under President Woodrow Wilson. Appeared in movies, and was legal counsel for Twentieth Century Fox Studios.

ARTHUR J. MAURER

Composer of "Amelia, Queen of the Air." At about age 30 he brought his family from Ohio and homesteaded in northeastern Wyoming, where he was a prospector as well as a writer and composer of music. His love for the West is reflected in some of his songs: "Just An Old Miner's Trail in the Black Hills," and "Let Me Live In Old Montana."

MARIANNE MOORE (1887–1972)

Born St. Louis, Missouri. Recipient of many awards including the Shelley Memorial Award and the National Book Award. Decorated with the Cross of the Legion of Honor; Order Arts and Letters (France). National Institute of Arts and Letters gold medal, poetry. Author: *The Fables of La Fontaine* (translation) 1954; *Three Classic Tales,* (translation), 1963; *Tell Me, Tell Me,* 1966; *Complete Poems,* 1968.

MURIEL MORRISSEY

Sister of Amelia Earhart. Born in Kansas City, Kansas. Attended Saint Margaret's College in Toronto and Smith College in Northampton, Massachusetts. Earned degrees from both Radcliffe College and Harvard University. For many years she taught at Belmont High School in Medford, Massachusetts. Her first major published work was a biography about her sister entitled *Courage is the Price.* She has received numerous honors and awards, and continues to be involved in civic, professional, and philanthropic organizations.

HENRY M. NEELY

Lyricist. Collaborated with Harold A. Levey on "Lady Lindy We're All For You." No other biographical information available.

EILIS O'CONNELL

Cork artist. Born in Derry, Ireland. Studied at the Crawford School of Art, Cork, from which she received a Diploma of Fine Art in Sculpture. Fine Art Awards include: Cork Arts Society Award in painting (1976); Cork Arts Society Award in Sculpture (1977); N.C.E.A. Award of Distinction in Sculpture (1977); The Mont Kavanagh Award for Environmental Art (1980); The Guinness Peat Aviation Award for Emerging Artists (1981); and a Fellowship for the British School in Rome from the Northern Arts Council (1983). Recent exhibits 1983 include a one-man exhibition of sculpture and wall pieces at The David Hendricks Gallery, Dublin, and "Women in Art," Wexford Art Centre, County Wexford.

PAULINE OLIVEROS

Associate Professor at the University of California San Diego, where she is head of the Center for Music Experiment and Related Research. In 1961 she was awarded the Pacifica Foundation Prize. A Guggenheim Fellow 1972–1973, she has written commissioned works for leading instrumentalists and singers.

MICKEY PARMAN

One of the first full-time women sports editors on a daily newspaper in the U.S., *The Atchison Globe* where she had her own column, "Sports Roamer." She has been with them for over twenty years, and now writes a column, "This is My World, Too." She is also a writer of fiction and poetry.

H.I. PHILLIPS (1889–1965)

Harry Irving Phillips began his newspaper career as a cub reporter for the *New Haven Register* and eventually became the Managing Editor. His first column "The Globe Trotter" appeared daily on the editorial page of the *New York Globe* beginning in 1917. When the *Globe* merged with the *New York Sun*, Phillips stayed on and began writing "The Sun Dial" (a column begun by Don Marquis). Known for his acerbic commentary, he often illustrated his columns with cartoons and laced his prose with puns. He is the author of *Private Purkey in Love and War,* and *On White or Rye.*

BEN PINCHOT

Photographer. Graduated from City College and the Columbia School of Mines. Deciding Engineering was not his forte, he went into partnership with a photographer in Greenwich Village. Several years later he opened his own photographic studio on Fifth Avenue, New York City. He specialized in portraits of writers, artists, and dancers. Pinchot also collaborated with his wife, Ann Pinchot, on two novels.

BRENDA PUTNAM (1890–1975)

Studied modeling and drawing at the Boston Museum of Fine Arts. Studied sculpture at the Art Students League of New York City with James Earle Fraser, and in Florence, Italy with Libero Andreotti. Her work is permanently represented at Folger Shakespeare Library, Washington, D.C., and at Brookgreen Gardens, Murrells Inlet, South Carolina. Her bust of Pablo Casals is in the collection of The Hispanic Society of America. She was the recipient of many awards, including the Barnett Prize of the National Academy of Design.

CHARLES ARTHUR RIDGWAY (b. 1878 d.   )

Composer, concert pianist, accompanist, and teacher. Founded the Dayton, Ohio Conservatory of Music in 1913. His compositions include the music for a children's play "Snickerty Nick and The Giant" by Julia Ellsworth Ford, based on Oscar Wilde's story "The Selfish Giant"; a Cantata, "I Will Extol Thee"; an Opera, "Jack of Hearts" and a musical setting of Kathryn Peck's poem "Traffic," dedicated to Lawrence Tibbett. About 1930, Mr. Ridgway accepted the directorship of the music department of the Harrison-Wallach Studios in Los Angeles and he lived in California for a number of years.

WILL ROGERS (1879–1935)

Immensely popular entertainer and homespun philosopher, roving ambassador and spokesman of common folk everywhere who "never met a man he didn't like." Born William Penn Adair Rogers, Colagh Indian Territory (Oklahoma). In 1917 he starred with the Ziegfeld Follies. His popularity with the advent of sound spread to other media, radio and the press. He declined a nomination for the governorship of Oklahoma, but he served as Mayor of Beverly Hills. A tribute to his achievements was paid in the 1952 film biography *The Story of Will Rogers*. His son, Will Rogers, Jr., played the title role in this film.

JOHN ROOD (1902–1974)

Minneapolis sculptor-writer. Began wood carving as a hobby during a summer in France. In his wood panels, "Pioneers In Progress" and "Spirit of Progress" he attempted to show the drive, energy, adaptability, resourcefulness, and patience which he felt were "in a large sense, attributes of women—all things eternal and basic."

HELEN B. SCHLEMAN

Began her long association with Purdue University in 1934 as Director of the first Women's Resident Hall, later serving as Dean of Women until her retirement in 1968. During World War II she served in the SPARS (U.S. Coast Guard) as an Executive Officer and Director, attaining the rank of Captain U.S.C.G.R. She has received a number of awards for her distinguished service to her country and community, including a citation from The Secretary of the Navy and the Gold Medallion Award from Purdue University.

WALTER RICHARD SICKERT (1860–1942)

English artist born in Munich. In 1883 he worked in Paris with Degas, with whom he shared an interest in theatre. Adopted from him the method of painting from drawings, memory, or photographs instead of on location. The elements of Sickert's style came from many sources—from Whistler he derived the method of painting in a narrow range of low tones. He shared with the Impressionists their concern for structure and their gift for design. In his etchings, he continued the tradition of Hogarth and Rowlandson. Much of his writing was published posthumously in *A Free House* (1947).

EDWARD STEICHEN (1879–1973)

Born in Luxembourg, he immigrated to America with his parents at an early age. His first photograph was a study of a cat in the window of his mother's millinery shop in Milwaukee. At age 15, he became an apprentice at the American Lithographing Company. Later he organized the Milwaukee Art Students League. In 1908, an influential periodical, *The Century,* published an article called "Progress in Photography" with special reference to his work. He was director of the Department of Photography at the Museum of Modern Art in New York City from 1947 until 1962. During this period he developed the most popular photography exhibit in history—"The Family of Man," a collection of some 500 photographs of men, women, and children by photographers from all over the world. The exhibit was viewed by people in more than 37 countries.

BRYNJULF STRANDENAES (1890–1952)

A painter of landscapes and portraits, he was for some years uncertain whether to turn to music or painting in his native Norway. Strandenaes came to America at an early age. Portraiture was a primary interest of the artist. Influenced by both the moderns—Sargent and Zorn, and the old masters—Veronese, Tintoretto, Velasquez, and Van Dyke. He painted portraits of King Haakon of Norway, opera singers Kirsten Flagstag and Lawrence Tibbett, as well as film star Gloria Swanson. The artist maintained a studio on West 57 Street in New York City, but in 1951, a debilitating illness sent him home to Oslo where he died.

CLARA TRENCKMANN STUDER (1897–1979)

Aviation writer. First editor of the first publication produced by the Ninety-Nines, Inc., *Airwoman,* serving in that capacity until 1936. She worked for *The Brooklyn Daily Eagle,* and was author of *Sky Storming Yankee,* the story of Glenn Hammond Curtiss.

ALFRED LORD TENNYSON (1809–1892)

Poet Laureate of England, often regarded as the chief representative of the Victorian age in poetry. He was deeply influenced by Byron and the Lincolnshire countryside where he was born. In 1827 he entered Trinity College Cambridge, and in 1829 won a gold medal for his poem "Timbuctoo."

LOUISE THADEN (1905–1979)

Friend of Amelia Earhart. She was a founding member of the Ninety-Nines in 1929, the first women's pilot organization in the United States. Mrs. Thaden was the first woman to win the famed Bendix Transcontinental Air Race, 1936, and in this same year captured the coveted Harmon Trophy. She was a writer of prose and poetry. Her autographed copper wings are on the famous Aviator's Wall, Mission Inn, Riverside, California.

LOWELL THOMAS (1892–1981)

Widely known for his radio broadcasts and movie newsreels during the Nineteen Thirties. Earned both a Bachelor of Science degree and a Master of Arts degree by age 20. A world traveler and adventurer, Mr. Thomas was the author of over 50 books, including *With Lawrence of Arabia; History as You Heard It; Good Evening Everybody;* and *So Long Until Tomorrow.*

RICHARDS VIDMER (1898–1978)

Best known for his nationally syndicated column *Down In Front,* he was a writer and sports broadcaster. He counted among his close friends Lou Gehrig, Joe Lewis, Grantland Rice, and Babe Ruth. He was an officer and a pilot in both World War I and World War II. He wrote for *The Washington Post, The New York Times,* and *The New York Herald Tribune,* in which his column appeared.

FRANCES ALICE WARD

She was a resident of Evanston, Illinois, when her poem to Amelia Earhart was written, in 1937. No further biographical information available.

FAY GILLIS WELLS

First woman member of the Caterpillar Club, having jumped from a disabled aircraft to save her life, September 1, 1929; a co-founder with Amelia Earhart and a charter member of the Ninety-Nines, now an international organization of more than 6,300 women pilots; first American woman pilot to fly in the Soviet Union. Presently co-general chairman of the International Forest of Friendship, a gift to America on her 200th birthday from the city of Atchison, Kansas, and the Ninety-Nines.

WILLIAM ALLEN WHITE (1868–1944)

Known as the Sage of Kansas. From 1895 until his death, he was editor of *The Emporia Gazette,* one of the most famous newspapers in the world. His writings included some collected letters in book form, and *Forty Years On Main Street,* a collection of his editorials. He was also author of an imaginative juvenile volume, *The Court of Bayville,* which critics labled as the literature of the future.

GILL ROBB WILSON (1893–1966)

Aviation columnist for *The New York Herald Tribune* and later editor of *Flying* Magazine for many years. During World War I he was a pilot with the 66th Escadrille (French), and the 163rd United States Army Air Squadron. In World War II he served as a war correspondent in Africa, Europe, and the Pacific.

ROBERT A. WINSLOW, JR. (1876–1963)

Born in London, Ontario, Canada. He worked first as a Telegraph messenger and later as a Telegraph operator. Also he worked as a court reporter in Hartford, Connecticut, and was later appointed Secretary of the Judiciary Committee of Connecticut (1923–1941). He was an avid sportsman. Enjoyed the writings of Emily Dickinson and Charles Dickens, and he frequently wrote poetry.

ROBERT YORK (1909–1975)

Minneapolis-born artist. Was influenced and encouraged by J.N. 'Ding' Darling. He worked on the *Chicago Tribune* and helped produce the syndicated comic strip "Harold Teen." Served as an artist in the United States Army Air Force. From 1937 to 1974, he was Editorial cartoonist for *The Louisville Times,* and during these years was recipient of the William Allen White Award and the Pulitzer Prize. He was truly an "artist's cartoonist."

Selected Bibliography

Books by Amelia Earhart:

20 hrs 40 mins—Our Flight in the Friendship. Putnam's Sons, New York-London, 1928. Reprint: Arno Press, New York, 1980.

Fun Of It—Random records of my own flying and women in aviation. Brewer, Warren & Putnam, New York, 1932. Reprints: Academy Chicago, Chicago, 1977. Gale Research Company, Detroit, 1975. Foreign language edition: *Plaisir des Ailes.* Gallimard-Paris, 1932; translation by R. Brua. Braille: Cleveland Chapter, American Red Cross, 1936; transcribed and presented by Pauline C. Votteler.

Last Flight. Harcourt, Brace & Company, New York, 1937. Reprint: Harbrace (paperback edition), Harcourt Brace, New York, 1965. Foreign language editions: *Denier Vol.* Gallimard, Paris, 1938; translated by Andhree Valliant. *Sista Flygningen.* Bokforlag, Stockholm, 1939; translated by T.V. Scheutz. *Az Utolso Ut.* Reva, Budapest, 1939, 1940, 1941; translated by Kosaryni Rez Lola. Romanian edition. Fundatia Pentru Si Arta, Bucharest, 1939.

Other selected reading:

Courage Is the Price by Muriel Earhart Morrissey. McCormick-Armstrong, Wichita, 1963. A biography and family chronicle.

Amelia Earhart by Nevin Bell. Albany Press (Heron Books), London, 1970; with Historical Appendix. A biography.

Soaring Wings; A Biography of Amelia Earhart by George Palmer Putnam. Harcourt Brace, 1939.

National Library Services For the Blind and Physically Handicapped, The Library of Congress, Washington, D.C.:

Amelia Earhart First Lady of the Air. BRA-09189, Jerry Seibert.

Famous American Women. TB 04103, Hope Stoddard. (Note: BRA = hand copies Braille; TB = disc)

Selections from *Cosmopolitan* Magazine while Amelia Earhart was its Aviation Editor:

"Try Flying Yourself." November 1928. Note this article was included in *Literary Treasures* of 1928.

"Man Who Tells the Fliers 'Go'!" May 1929.

"On the Floor of the Sea." November 1929.

"Mrs. Lindbergh." July 1930.

The following articles written by Amelia Earhart are in the American Institute of Aeronautics and Astronautics Collection, Library of Congress, Manuscript Division, Washington, D.C.:

"Poet's Corner"—Shall Hard Facts Give Way to Gentle Blandishments? *The Sportsman Pilot,* July 1929.

What Flying Is Teaching Women—An Interview with Amelia Earhart by A.A. Preciado. (Publication unknown/n.d. Box No. 24.)

"Women's Influence on Air Transport Luxury." *The Aeronautic Review,* March 1930. (Note: from a radio address by Miss Earhart . . . broadcast by the National Broadcasting Company in cooperation with the Aeronautical Chamber of Commerce.)

"The Most Traveled Road." Amelia Earhart, Vice-President, New York, Philadelphia and Washington Airways Corporation. *The National Aeronautic Magazine,* November 1930.

"Putting Air Travel Into Mass Production" by Amelia Earhart, Vice-President, Ludington Lines. *Aviation,* May 1931.

"Plane Clothes." Article by Amelia Earhart ca. 1928, included in *Harper's Bazaar*—100 years of the American Female. Edited by Jane Trahey. Copyright 1913–1967 by Hearst Corporation. Random House.

Additional reading from various publications:

She Has Certainly Earned It . . . Amelia—Our "Trail Blazer" by Phoebe Fairgrave Omlie. *The National Aeronautic Magazine,* January 1935.

"Amelias Have Changed Since Thackeray's 'Vanity Fair.'" (Note: no author given.) *U.S. Services* Magazine, June 1932.

"A.E." by Hart Wells. *U.S. Services* Magazine, June 1932.

The Society's Special Medal Awarded to Amelia Earhart—First Woman to Receive Geographic Distinction at Brilliant Ceremony in the National Capitol. *National Geographic* Magazine, September 1932.

Presentation of the Society of Woman Geographer's Gold Medal to Amelia Earhart. *Bulletin*—Society of Woman Geographers, June 1933.

"Miss Earhart Goes to the Play." Review by Amelia Earhart of "Ceiling Zero." *Stage,* July, 1935.

Letter written by Amelia Earhart to *The New York Herald Tribune* March 25, 1934—concerns the creation of Secretary of Transportation, written at the time of the Air Mail controversy (Note: letter appears in the Historical Appendix of *Amelia Earhart* by Nevin Bell listed elsewhere in this bibliography.)

"Ace-High Dishes—Amelia Earhart, feminine ace of the air, takes a successful flyer in waffles and Sunday night suppers" by Grace Turner. *This Week,* October 4, 1936.

"Philatelists Will Always Remember Amelia Earhart" by Admiral Jesse G. Johnson. *The American Philatelist* (The Journal of the American Philatelic Society), vol. 76, no. 9, June 1963.

Amelia Earhart—Friendship Flights.   *The Airpost Journal,* September 1963.

Amelia Earhart Commemorated by Special Surinam Stamps.   *Surinam Sun,* vol. 3, no. 3, June–July 1967.

Amelia Earhart—The Aviation Record of America's Most Famous Woman Pilot by Walter Curley, Librarian, Cardinal Spellman Philatelic Museum, Inc., Regis College, Weston, Mass., 1966. (Note: Bibliography with illustrations of stamp covers pertaining to her various flights.)

American Heroes of the 20th Century.   Harold & Doris Faber, Random House, New York, 1967.

''Amelia Earhart's Legacy'' by Katherine A. Brick. *U.S. Lady* (The Service Family Journal), Washington, D.C., vol. 8, no. 3, July 1963.

Edited by Beverly Bohlinger Hegman

Designed by Gerard A. Valerio, Bookmark Studio

Composed in Garamond by BG Composition Inc., Baltimore, Maryland.

Printed on Warren's Lustro Enamel by the Collins Lithographing and Printing Company, Baltimore, Maryland.